MW01609242

Windows 10 Microsoft Edge: The Complete Guide

Copyright © 2015.

What is Microsoft Edge?

Microsoft Edge is the new default browser of the Windows 10 operating system. Formerly known by its code name, Project Spartan, Microsoft Edge provides the user with a more personal and rewarding web experience.

Features

Web Note

There's no need to interrupt your browsing to search for a notepad and pen to jot down notes.

With Web Note, you can now write directly on the web pages that you're browsing by selecting Make a Web Note ⬚ .

After clicking on Make a Web Note ⬚ , the following menu will come up. (refer to the screenshot below)

Select the best writing option to meet your needs. (refer to the screenshot below)

To write with the Pen ∇ , click on the Pen icon ∇ . Select the color and size you desire, then write using your touchscreen, touchpad, or mouse. (refer to the screenshot below)

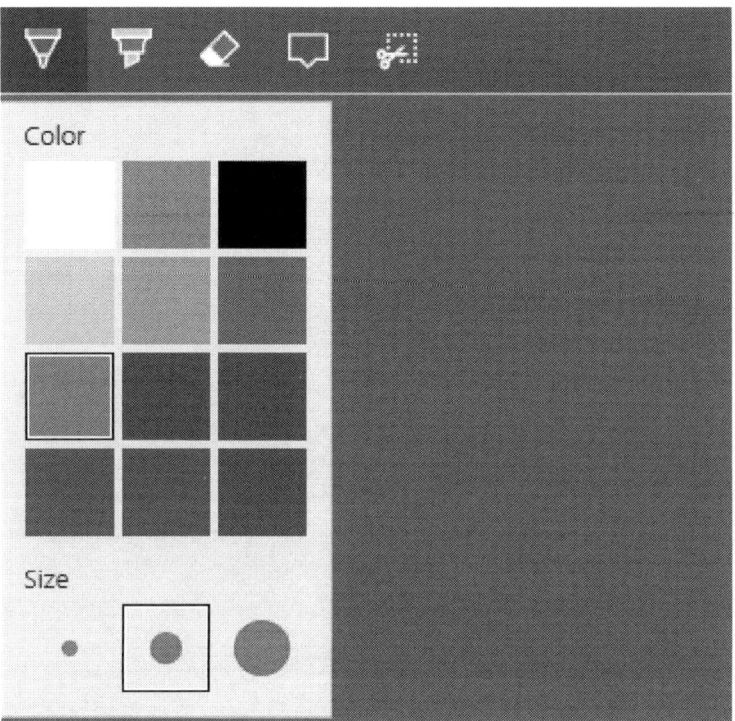

Here's an example of the writing done with the medium size pen tip in black ink. (refer to the screenshot below)

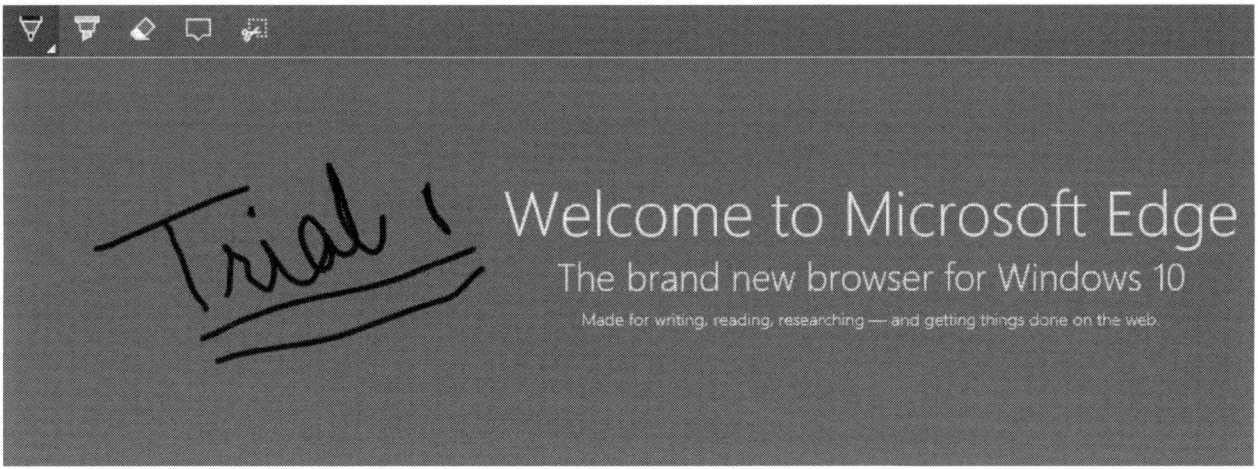

If there are portions of the web page that you'll like to single out for future reference, click on the Highlighter icon 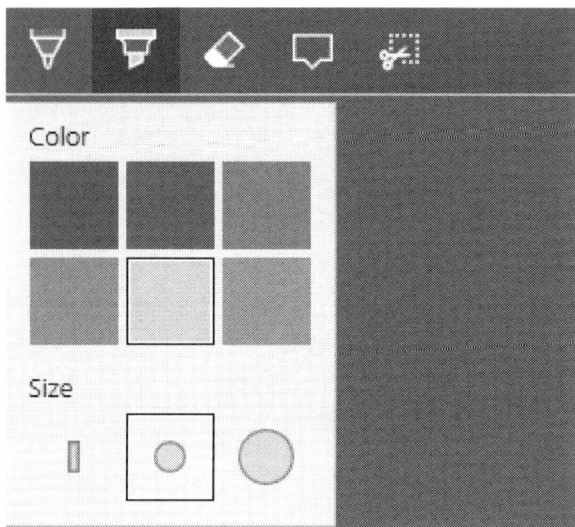. Select the color and shape you desire, then highlight the section(s) of the page using your touchscreen, touchpad, or mouse. (refer to the screenshot below)

Here's an example of an article that was highlighted using the small size highlighter tip in the color green. (refer to the screenshot below)

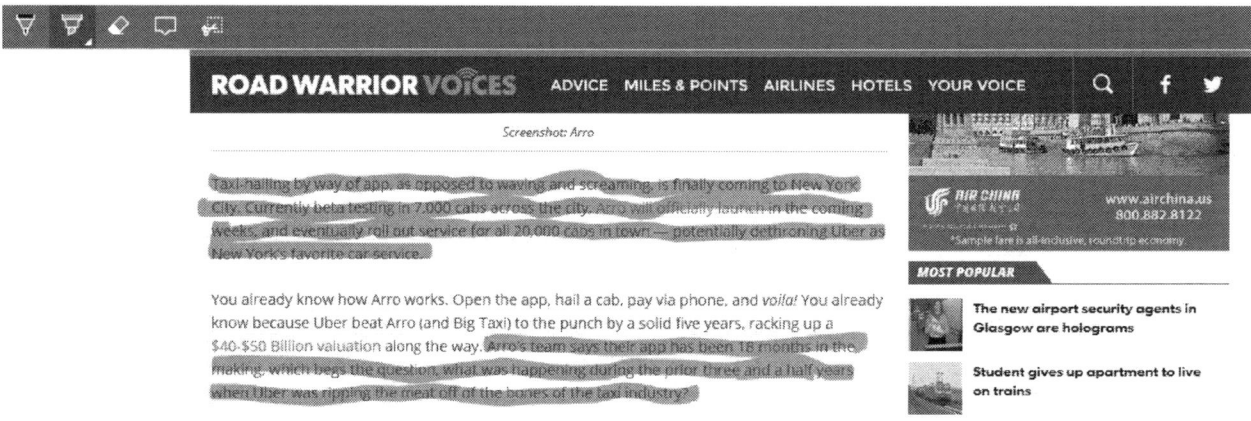

If you happen to make a mistake while using the Pen or Highlighter , you can erase it by clicking on the Eraser icon, then by clicking on Clear all ink. (refer to the screenshot below)

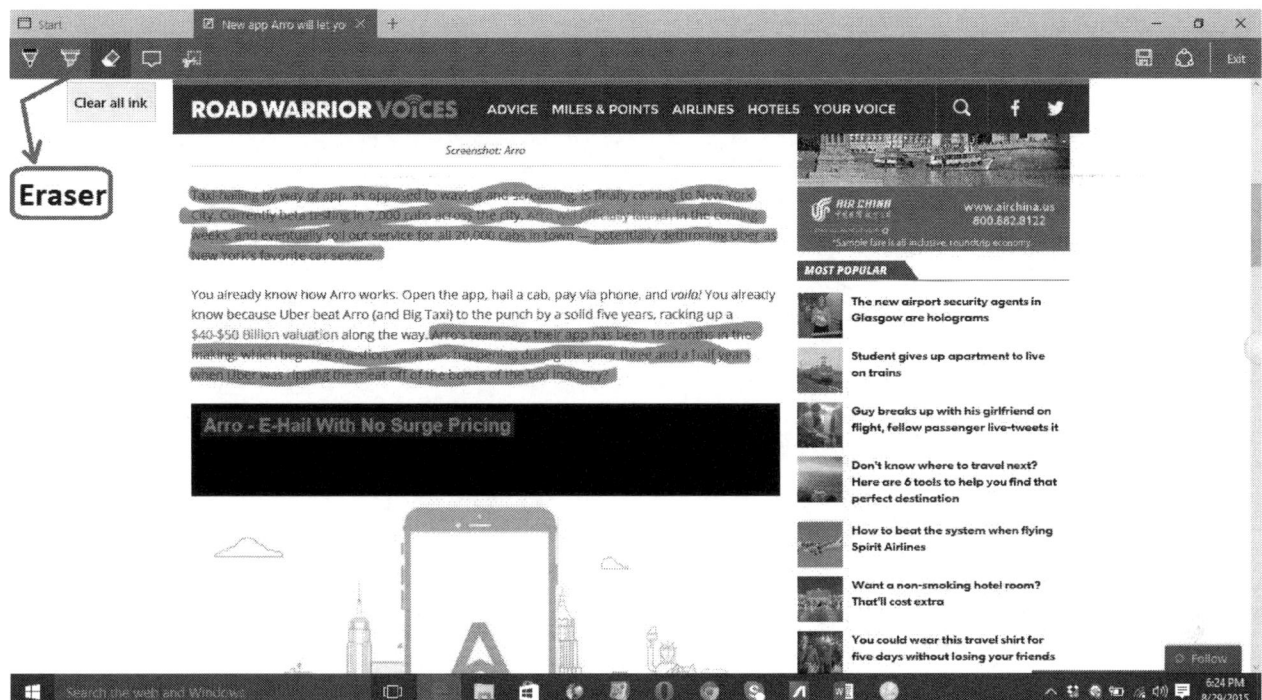

If you prefer simplicity over color coded notes, click on the Add a typed note icon to add captions to your page. Move the icon to the desired area of the page and type a note. (refer to the screenshot below)

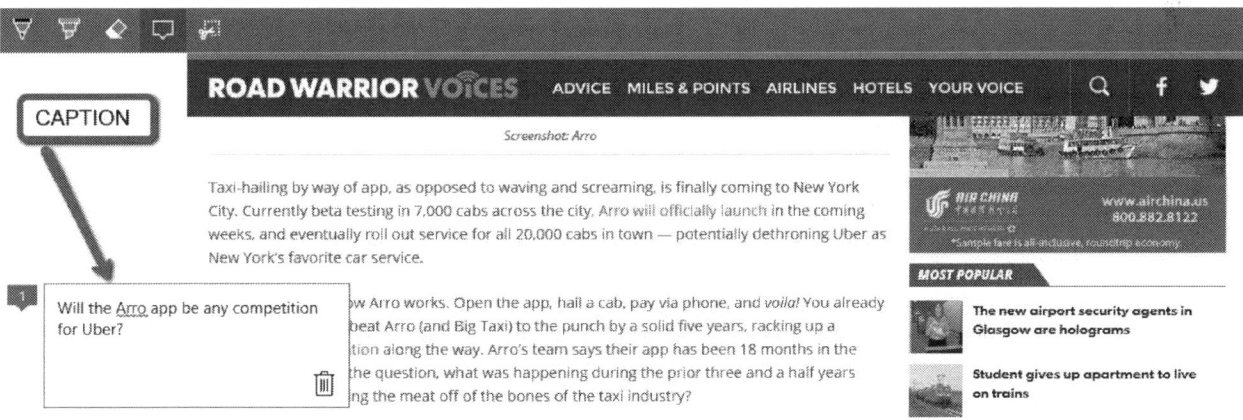

Instead of using the Pen, Highlighter, or Add a typed note options, you can simply clip the area(s) of the page you desire. Click on the Clip icon [icon]. Hold down the left mouse button or touchpad and drag to outline the section(s) you desire. If you're using a touchscreen, swipe to outline the region of your choice. (refer to the screenshot below)

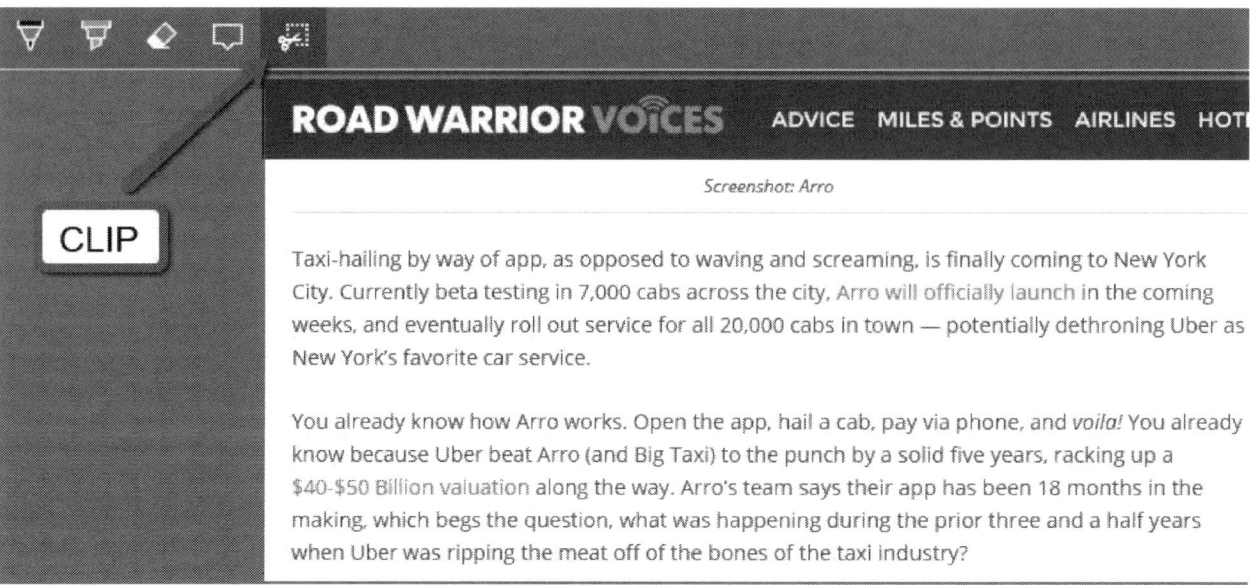

After taking your notes, you can also save your work for future reference using the Save Web Note icon [icon]. After clicking on the Save Web Note icon [icon], you'll be provided with three options as circled in red below. You can send your work to OneNote, or add it to your Favorites or Reading List. Additionally, you have the option of sharing it with others in your network using the Share icon [icon]. (refer to the screenshot below)

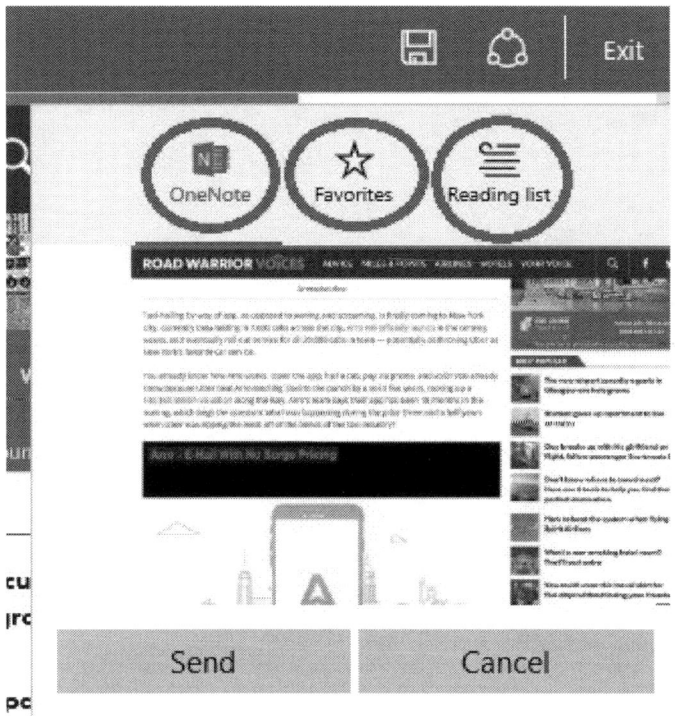

Reading List App

Besides the writing component of Microsoft Edge, there is the Reading List app that allows you to save interesting content and articles to read at a later time. Click on the Favorites icon ☆ , select the Reading List icon , change the title to your liking, and click on the Add button. (refer to the screenshot below)

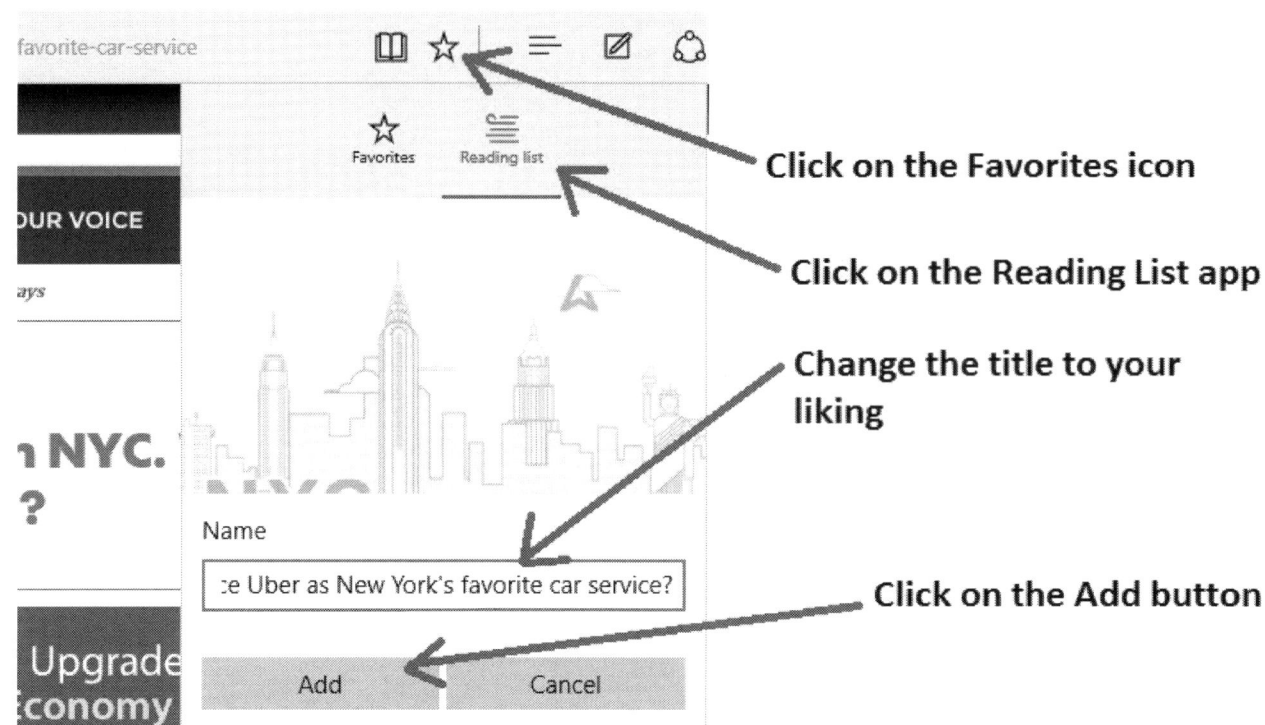

Click on the Favorites icon

Click on the Reading List app

Change the title to your liking

Click on the Add button

To gain access to the Reading List, click on the Hub icon 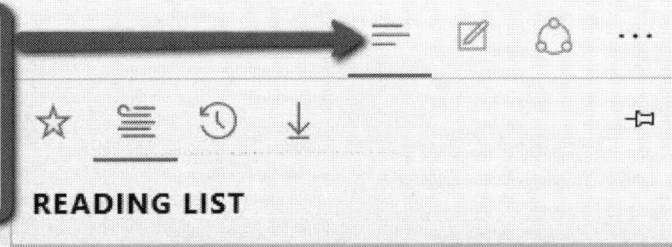 . You'll be presented with a chronological lineup of all the items you saved. (refer to the screenshot below)

Click on the Hub icon to gain access to the Reading List

This is a lineup of the articles that were saved in the Reading List app.

The list is presented with the most recent article that was added to the Reading List at the top.

READING LIST

Six women in best position to derail Serena Williams' calendar Slam
usatoday.com

Today

Six women in best position to derail Serena Williams' calendar Slam
usatoday.com

IRS needs to do more to fight income tax identity theft
usatoday.com

New app Arro will let you hail any yellow taxi in NYC. Will it replace Uber
roadwarriorvoices.com

Reuters

Once you've finished reading an article or web page, you can remove it from your Reading List by right clicking it and selecting remove. (refer to the screenshot below)

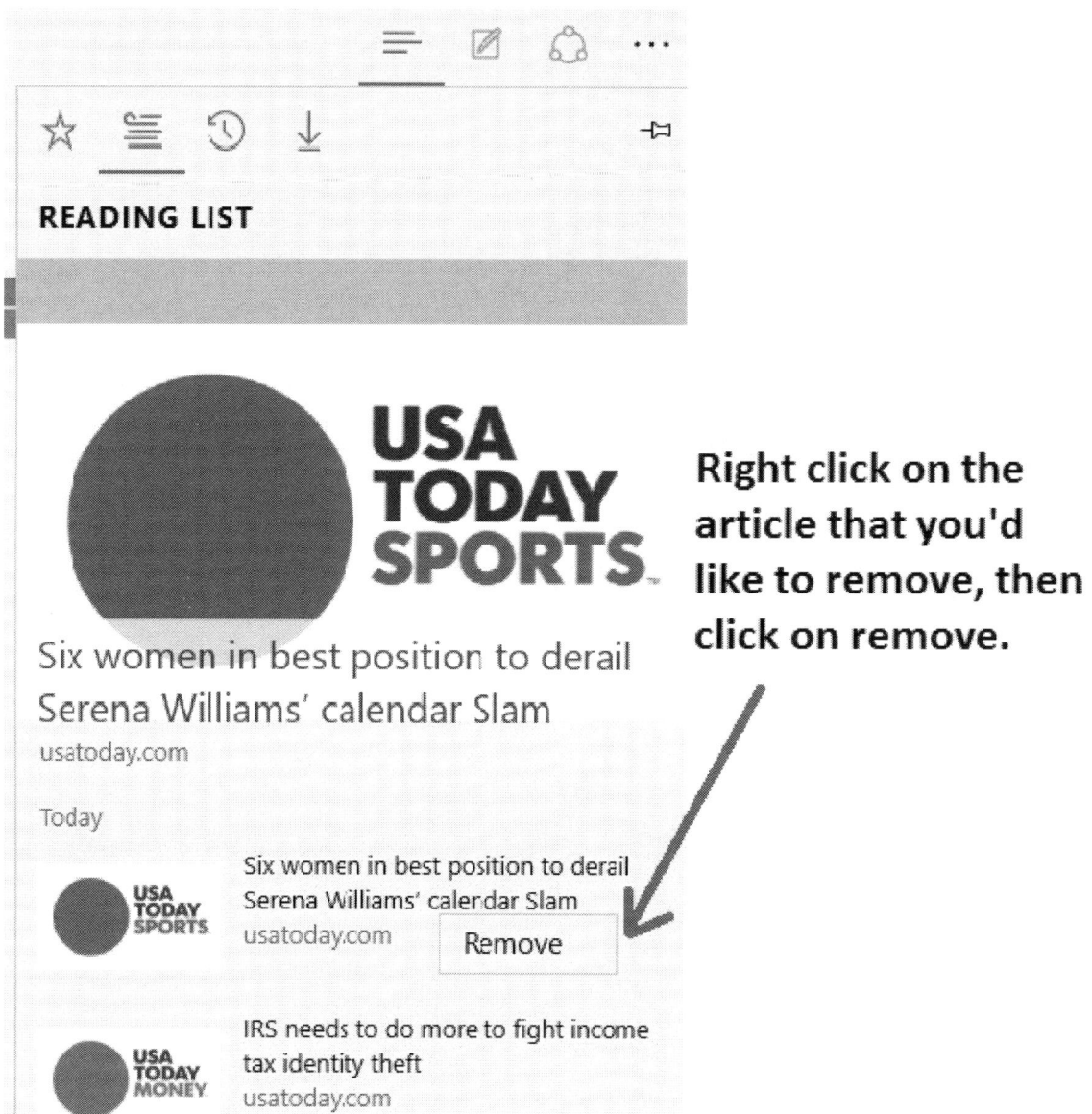

Items in the Reading List can be saved for temporary use, while those in Favorites can be saved for long-term use.

To save an item in Favorites, click on the Favorites icon ☆, enter the Name you desire, then click Add. (refer to the screenshot below)

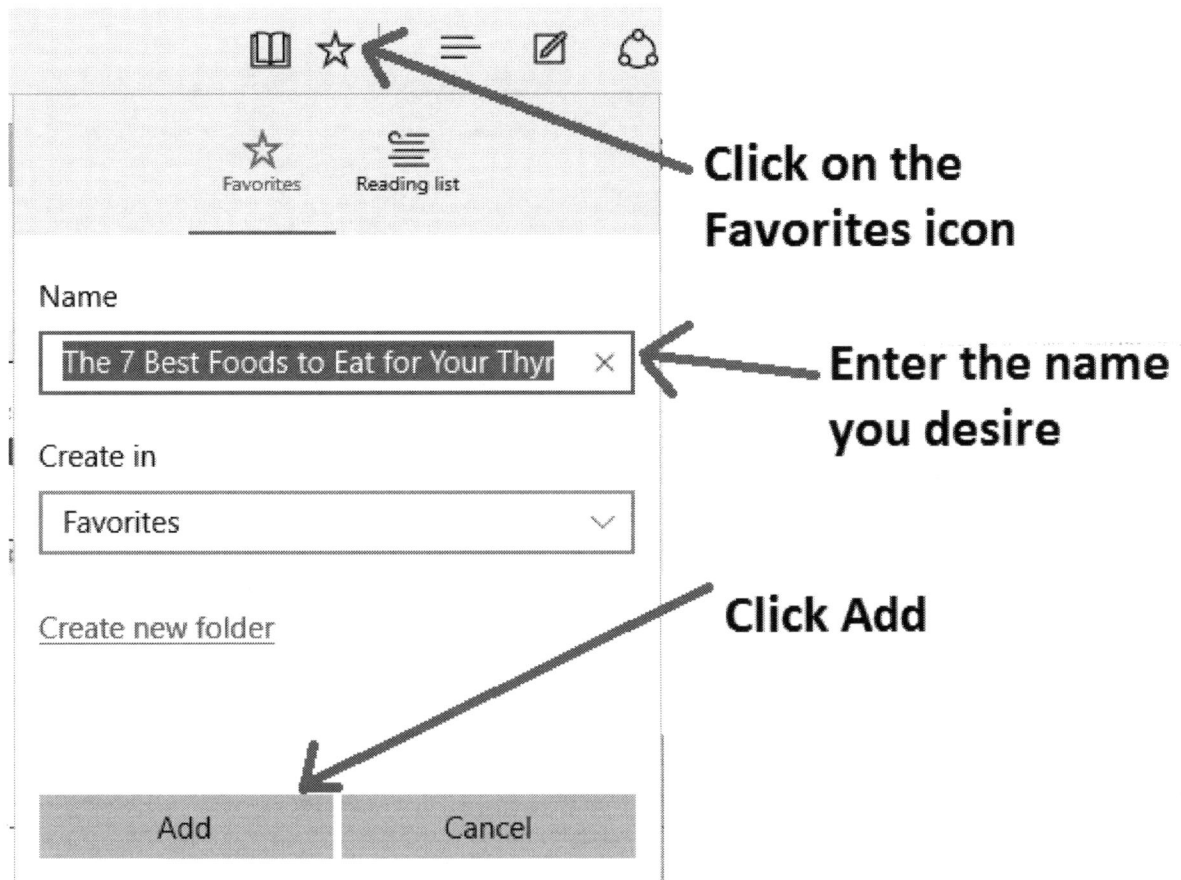

Click on the Favorites icon

Enter the name you desire

Click Add

If you decide to read right away and have a habit of multitasking, you can switch to Reading View ▥ to eliminate any distractions that may take you away from the content you actually want to read.

Here's an example of a web page in Reading View. (refer to the screenshot below)

© Eat This, Not That!

The 7 Best Foods to Eat for Your Thyroid and Metabolism

Eat This, Not That!
MSN

Tired? Stressed? Can't lose weight? You're not alone. In fact, you may be one of the millions of Americans suffering a chronic, undiagnosed health issue. It's called hypothyroidism: a condition that pumps the brakes on your metabolism because the master gland—your thyroid—isn't functioning at its prime.

Your thyroid is an unassuming butterfly-shaped gland in your neck that secretes all-im-

• • •

To change the style and font size of the web page, go to the More Actions icon _____, then click on Settings. (refer to the screenshot below)

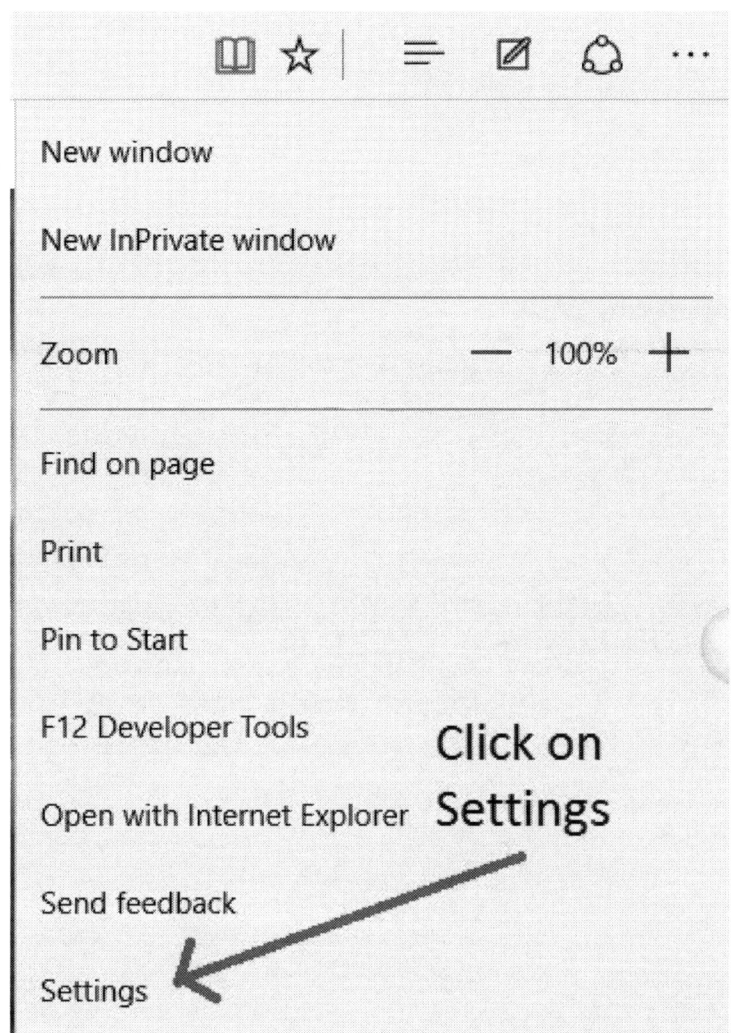

New window

New InPrivate window

Zoom   — 100% +

Find on page

Print

Pin to Start

F12 Developer Tools   Click on

Open with Internet Explorer   Settings

Send feedback

Settings

Choose a theme from the drop down menu. There are two options: Light and Dark. This changes the color of the Settings menu and address bar. (refer to the screenshot below)

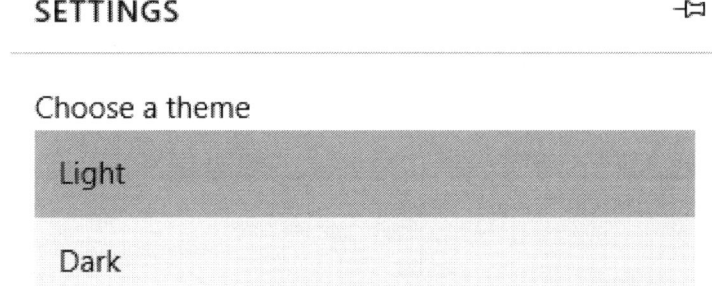

SETTINGS   ⊣⊐

Choose a theme

Light

Dark

Select the Reading view style and Reading view font size you desire. The style and font size features both have four options. The Reading view style options include Default, Light, Medium, and Dark. While the Reading view font size options are Small, Medium, Large, and Extra Large. (refer to the screenshots below)

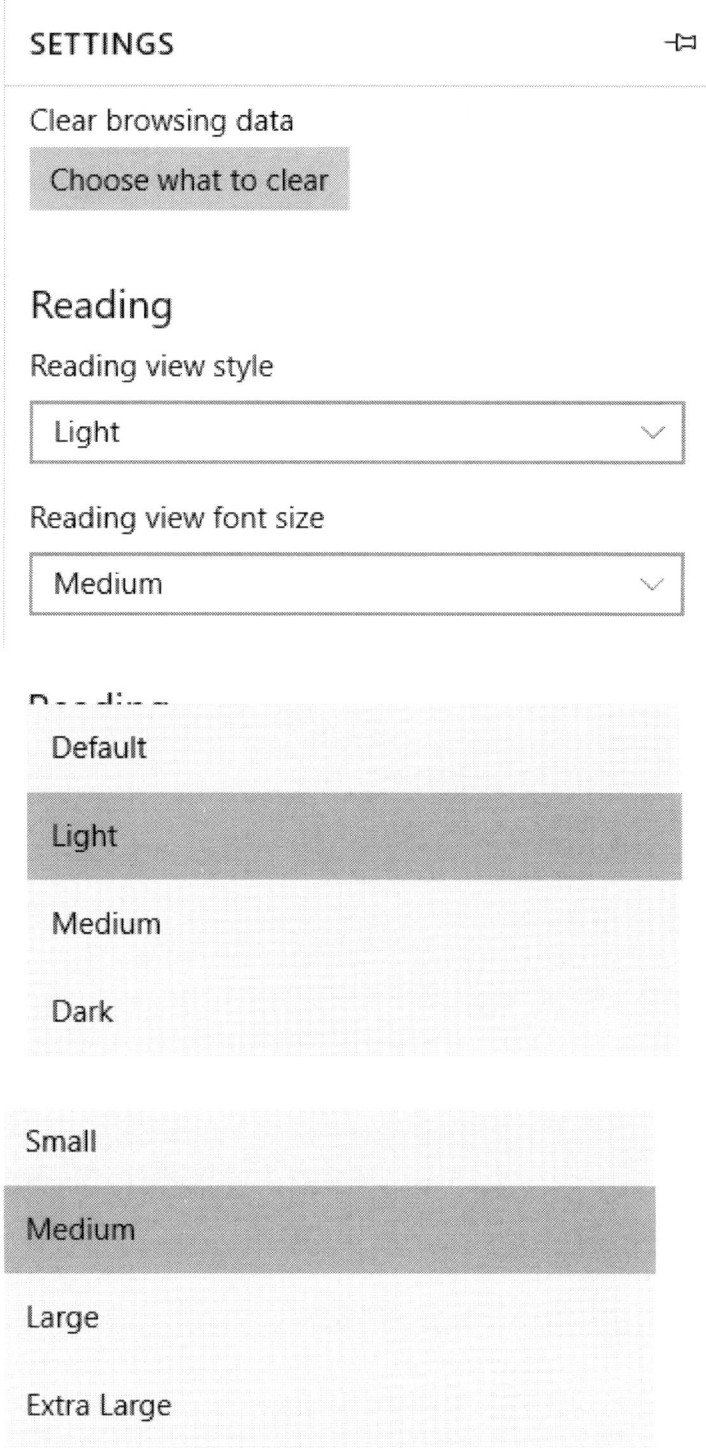

Downloads

To gain access to your Downloads, click on the Hub icon ≡, then click on the Downloads icon ↓. Under this section you'll see all the past downloads that you have completed in the Microsoft Edge browser. (refer to the screenshot below)

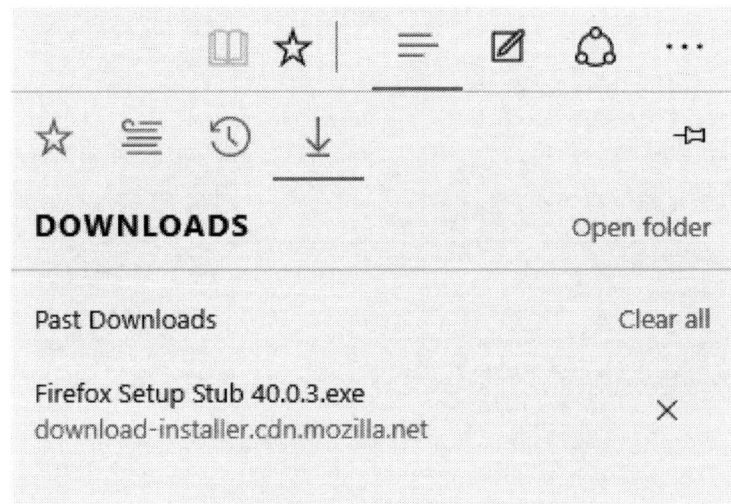

To access the folder with your Downloads, click on Open folder located on the right hand side of the DOWNLOADS heading. If you'd like to delete a specific download, click on the x located directly next to it. If you'd like to delete all of your Downloads, click on Clear all which is located at the top right hand corner of your Downloads list. (refer to the screenshot above)

PDF Documents

To save a PDF document, right click on the document and click on Save as. (refer to the screenshot below)

Once you click on Save as, you'll be prompted to save the document to your device. You can use the File name provided or rename it. (refer to the screenshot below)

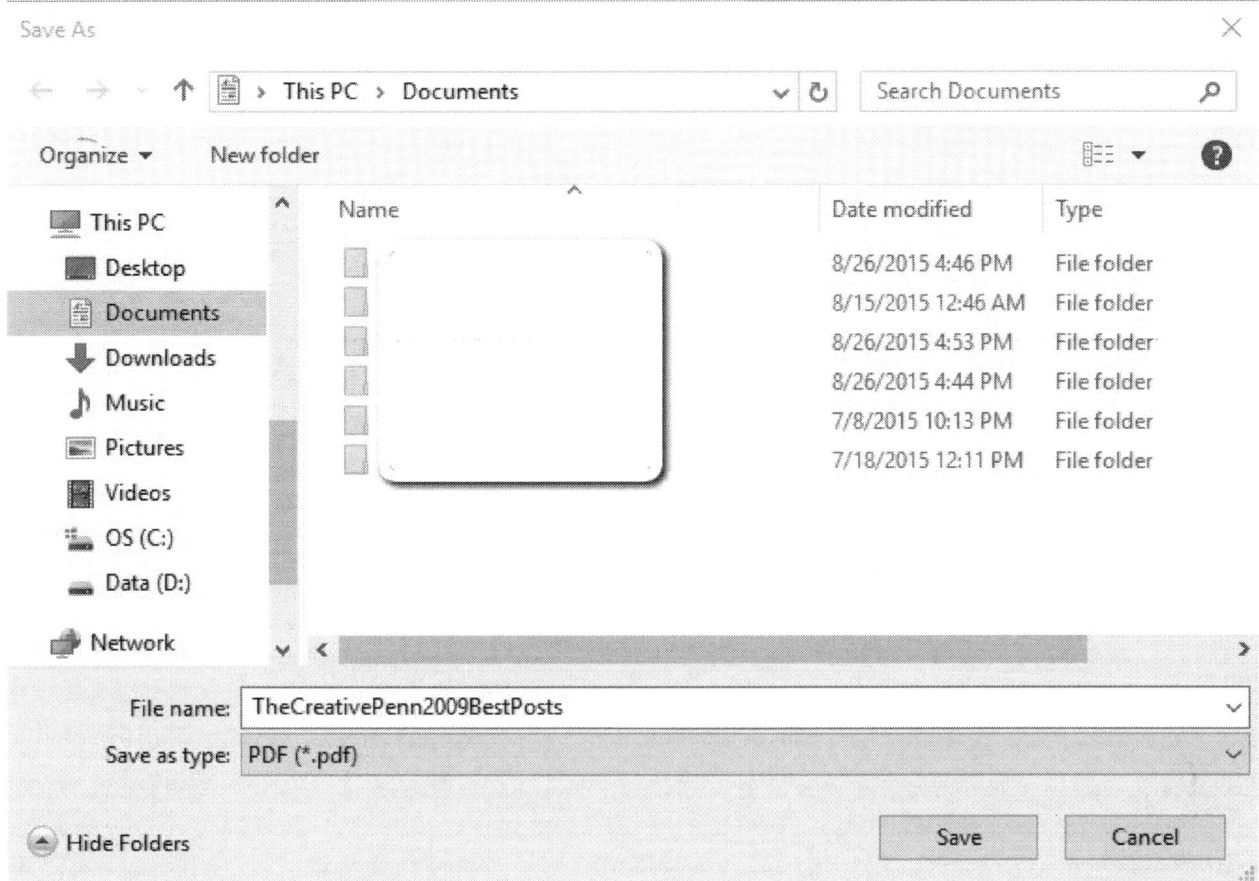

Tabs

With the Google Chrome and Firefox browsers you have the ability to switch the position of your tabs in a single window or convert a tab into a new window by dragging it out of the browser. However, Microsoft Edge doesn't allow you to rearrange the order of your tabs or convert tabs into new windows by using the dragging function. In order to convert a tab into a new window in Microsoft Edge, right click on the tab, then click on Move to new window. (refer to the screenshot below)

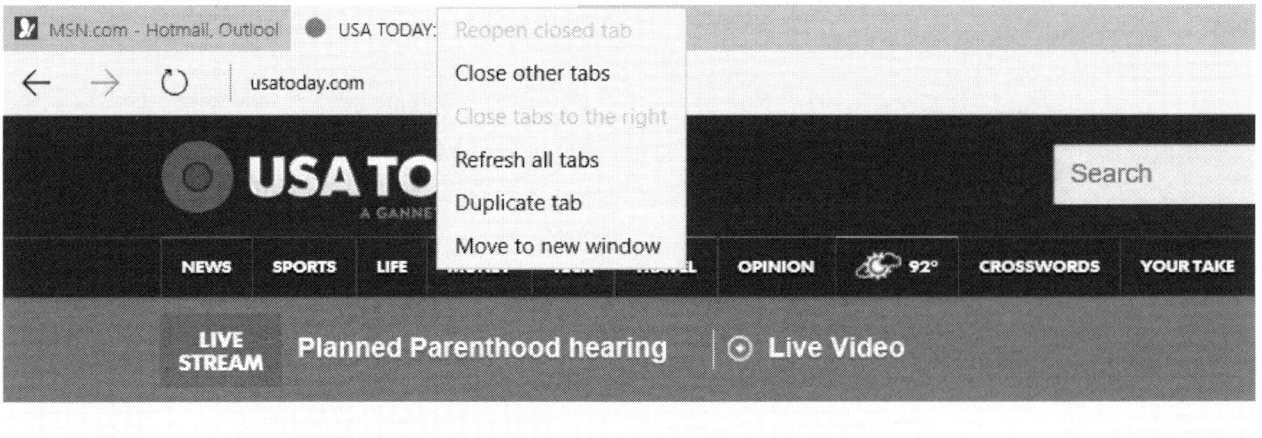

New Window and Private Browsing

To open a new window in Microsoft Edge, click on the More actions icon ____, then select New window. For private browsing, click on New InPrivate window. (refer to the screenshot below)

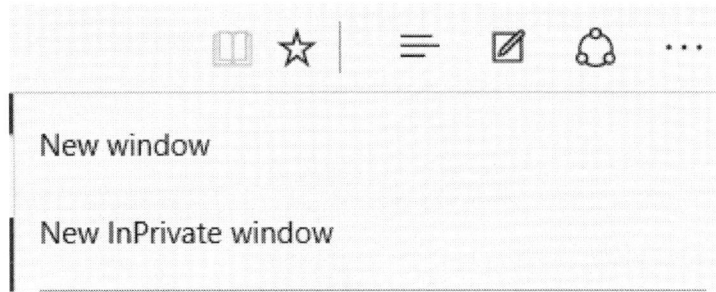

New window

New InPrivate window

In private browsing mode, your browsing history isn't saved on your device.

Zoom

To increase or decrease the size of a web page, use the Zoom feature. Click on the More actions icon

...

____, then go to Zoom. If you'd like to increase the size of the web page, select the Zoom in icon ➕ .

If you'd like to decrease the size of the web page, select the Zoom out icon ➖ .

Pin to Start

To pin a web page as a tile to the Start menu or screen, click on the More actions icon , then scroll down to Pin to Start. To view all the web pages that you have pinned to the Start menu or screen click on the Start button. (refer to the screenshot below of websites pinned to the Start menu)

To name your group of pinned websites, click in the area to which the red arrow is pointing in the screenshot above, enter the name you desire, and hit Enter. If you decide that the name you selected is no longer relevant to your group of websites, you can change the name by clicking on the icon with the two lines [==], then by typing the new name and hitting Enter.

To unpin a tile from the Start menu, right click on the tile and click on Unpin from Start. To resize a tile, right click on the tile and hover over the Resize option and select the Small or Medium option. To turn a live tile off, right click on the tile and click on Turn live tile off. (refer to the screenshot below)

If you'd like to switch from the Start menu to the Start screen, click on the Start button, then click on Settings. Select Personalization, then click on Start. Under the heading Use Start full screen, slide the button to the On position. (refer to the screenshot below)

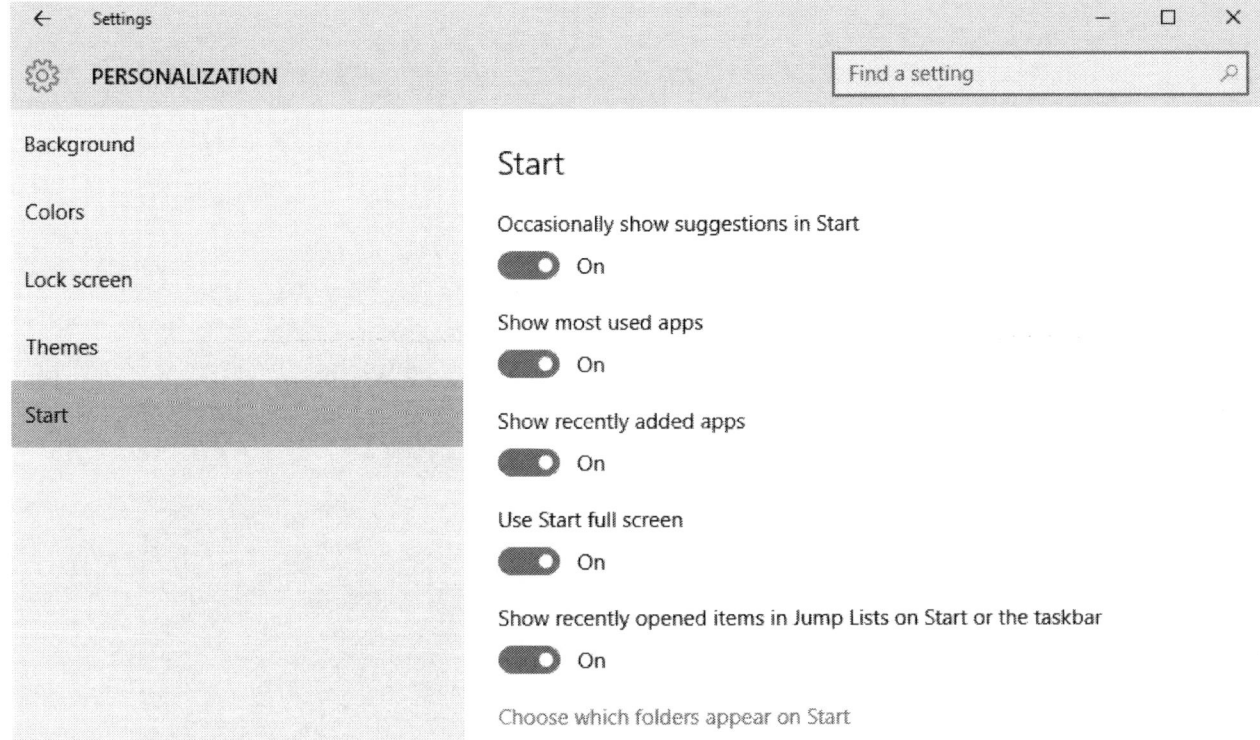

To resize the Start menu, move the cursor to the edge of the Start menu and drag the cursor in or out to shrink or expand.

Here's a screenshot of the Start menu at its regular size.

Here's a screenshot of the Start menu expanded.

Cortana

Search engines can be put to rest once Cortana is put to work. Instead of going to search engines such as Google, Yahoo, or Bing, you can simply go to Cortana and make your request.

To set up Cortana with your personal preferences, click in the search box in the bottom left hand corner of your screen. (refer to the screenshot below)

After clicking in the search box, Cortana will present you with a few starter interests. (refer to the screenshot below)

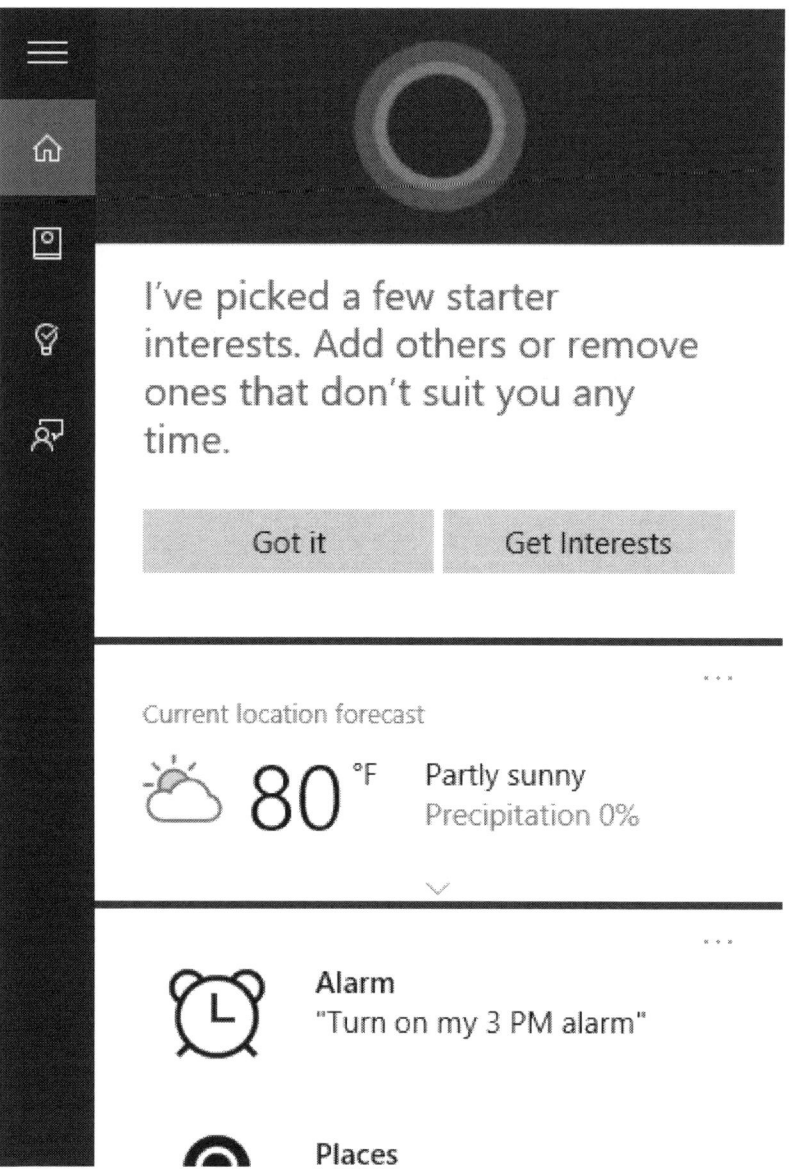

You can add or remove the interests to suit your personal needs. Find out about the weekly weather forecast, or if you'll encounter traffic on your way to work. Get your local news before heading out the door, or get the solution for the square root of a specific number. (refer to the screenshot below)

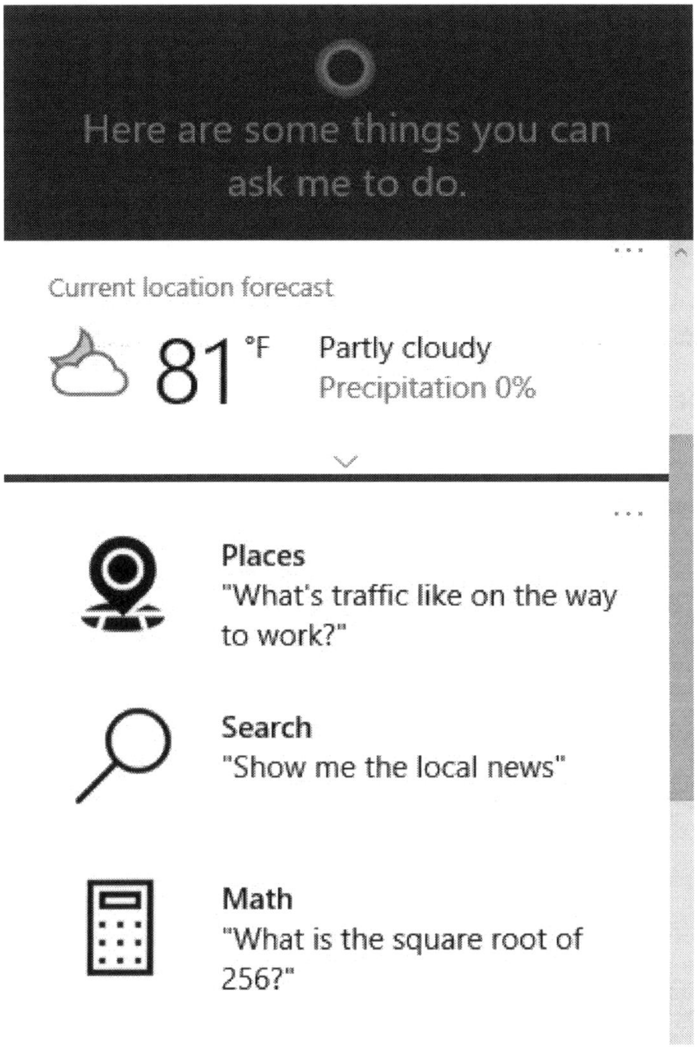

Here are some things you can
ask me to do.

Current location forecast

 81 °F   Partly cloudy
Precipitation 0%

Places
"What's traffic like on the way
to work?"

Search
"Show me the local news"

Math
"What is the square root of
256?"

If you're unsure of what interests you should select, click on Get Interests for a list of categories. (refer to the screenshot below)

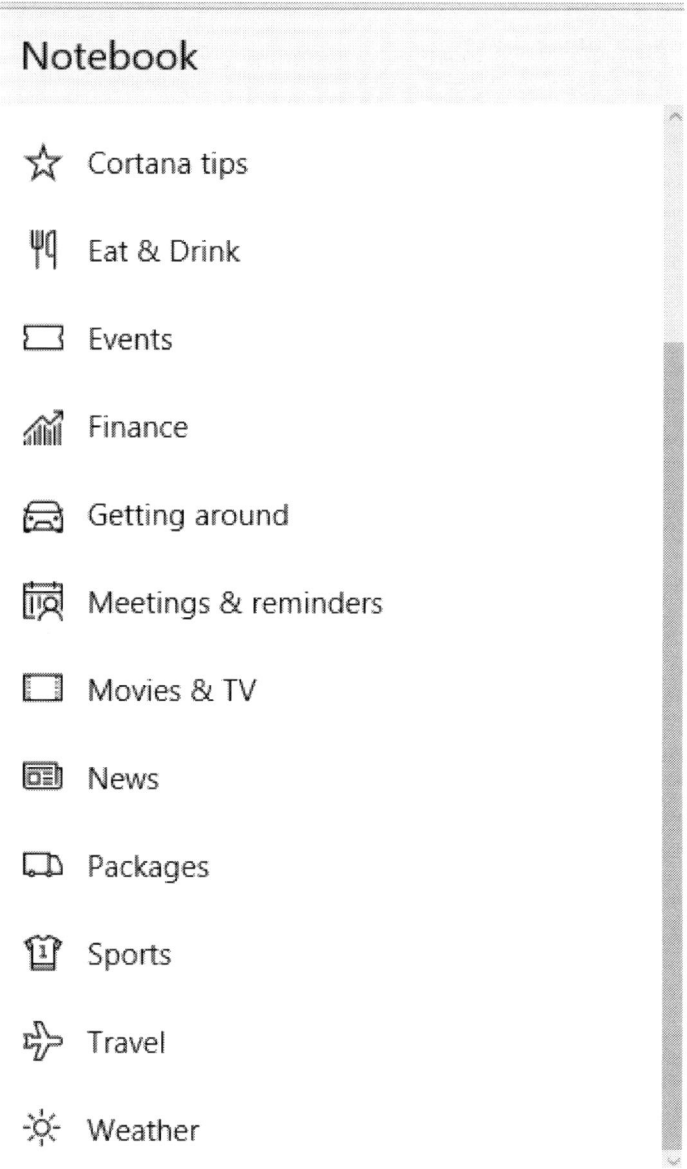

Do you have a dentist appointment, or a meeting with a business partner? You can set a reminder with

details such as the person, place, or time. To add a new reminder, click on the Add icon ⊞. (refer to the screenshot below)

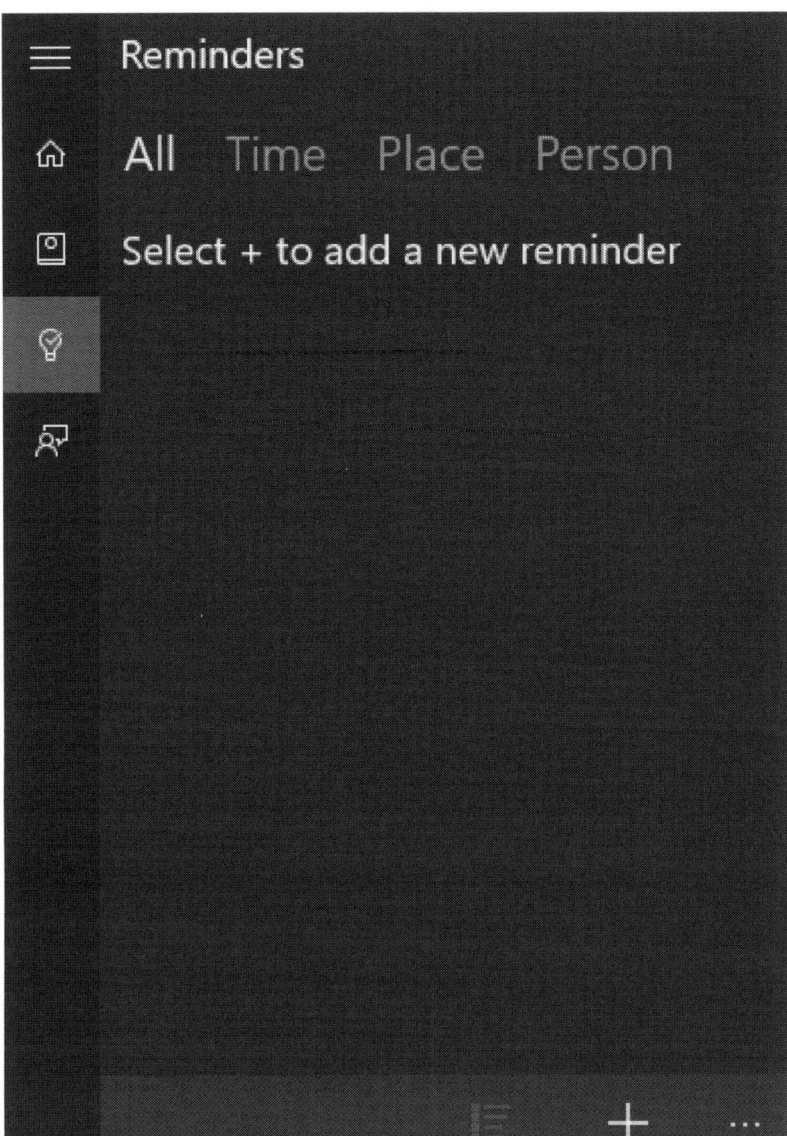

You'll be directed to the screen below and asked to fill out information about what you'd like to be reminded about. After entering the information, click on Remind. (refer to the screenshot below)

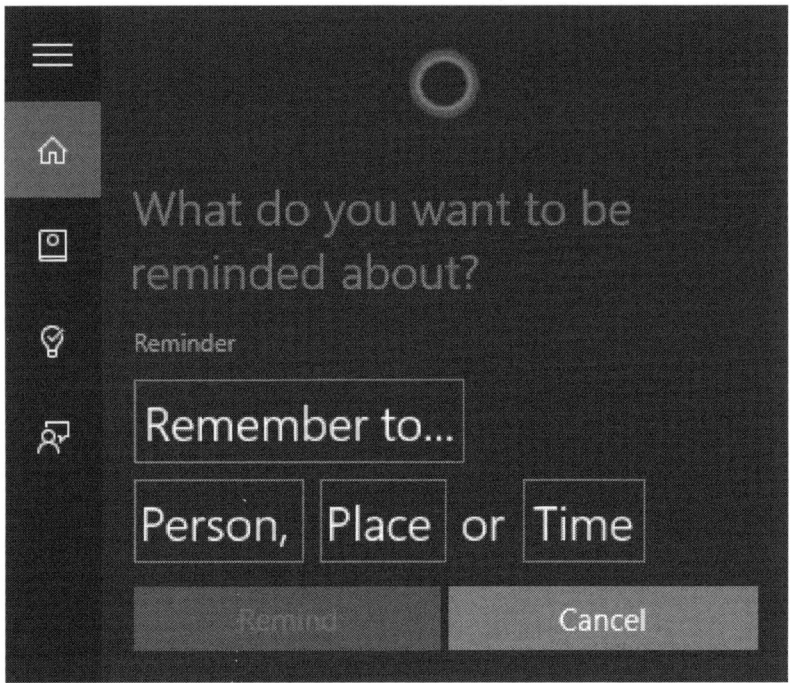

Now that you've set up Cortana to your liking, you can start using your digital personal assistant to help you manage your day to day activities. Type a question in the search box, or click on the Mic icon and talk.

Cortana FAQs

Is Cortana suitable for children?

You must have a Microsoft account in order to gain access to Cortana. If the Microsoft account being used is a child account that was created for a user under the age of 13, that person would be denied access. Cortana would inform the person that he/she must be a bit older in order to utilize that feature.

How can I change the name that Cortana calls me?

To change the name that Cortana calls you, open Cortana, go to Notebook , and click on About Me.

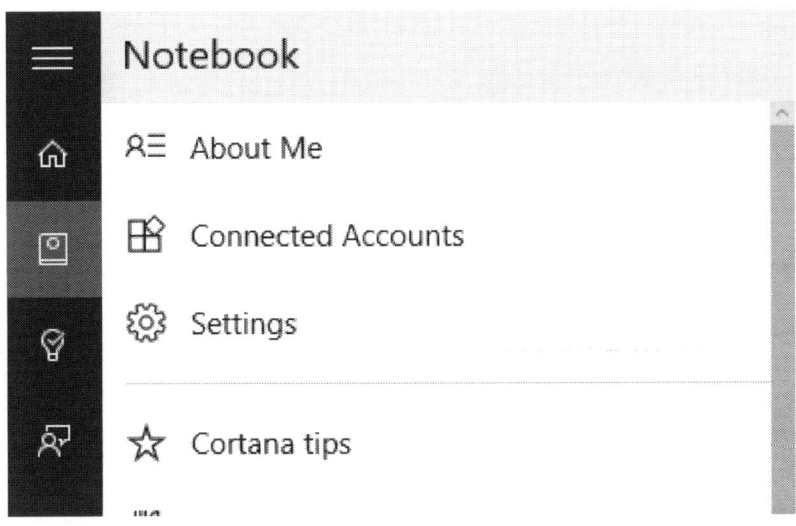

Click on Change my name.

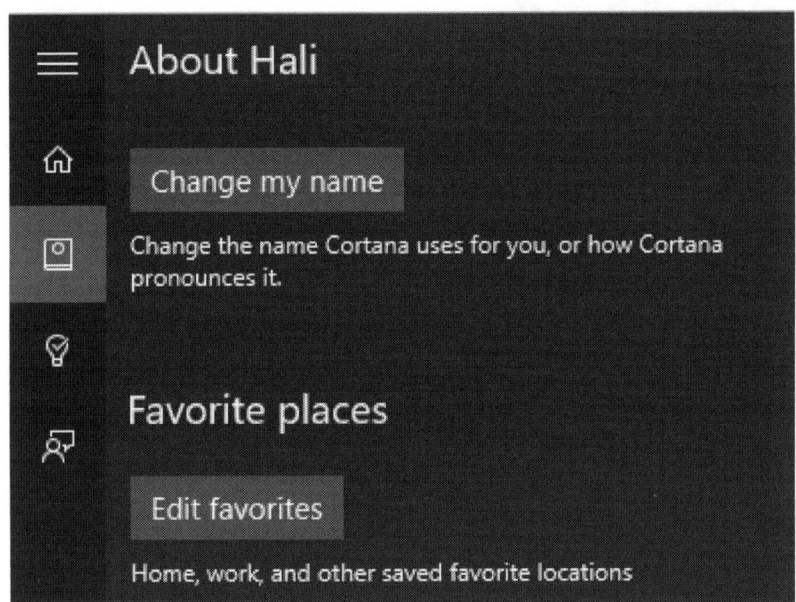

Type the name you desire, then click Enter.

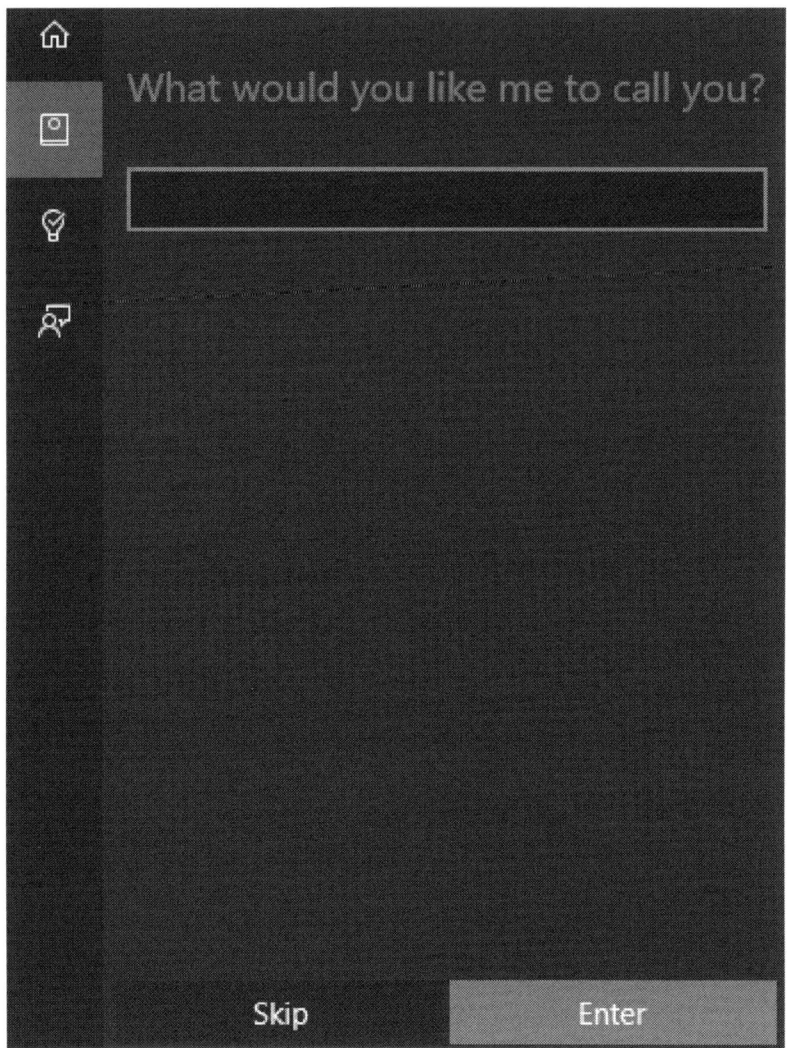

How can I manage my personal information that Cortana has stored?

If you saved information about your favorite places or specific interests you can remove or update these

items by clicking on the Notebook icon located on the Cortana menu, then by clicking on the

About me option. Choose the item you'd like to delete and click on the Trashcan icon to remove it.

For example, if you selected Seafood as one of your Cuisine preferences and you no longer wanted to have it as a preference, here's what you would do.

Go to Notebook

 Eat & Drink

Click on the Eat & Drink category

Cuisine preference

 + Add a cuisine

Scroll down to Cuisine preference and click on Seafood

Click on the Trashcan icon at the bottom of the page to remove it from your preferences.

You can also go directly to the Bing.com dashboard to clear your personal information. To do so, click on

the Notebook icon , then click on Settings and go to Manage what Cortana knows about me in the cloud.

You'll be directed to the following page:

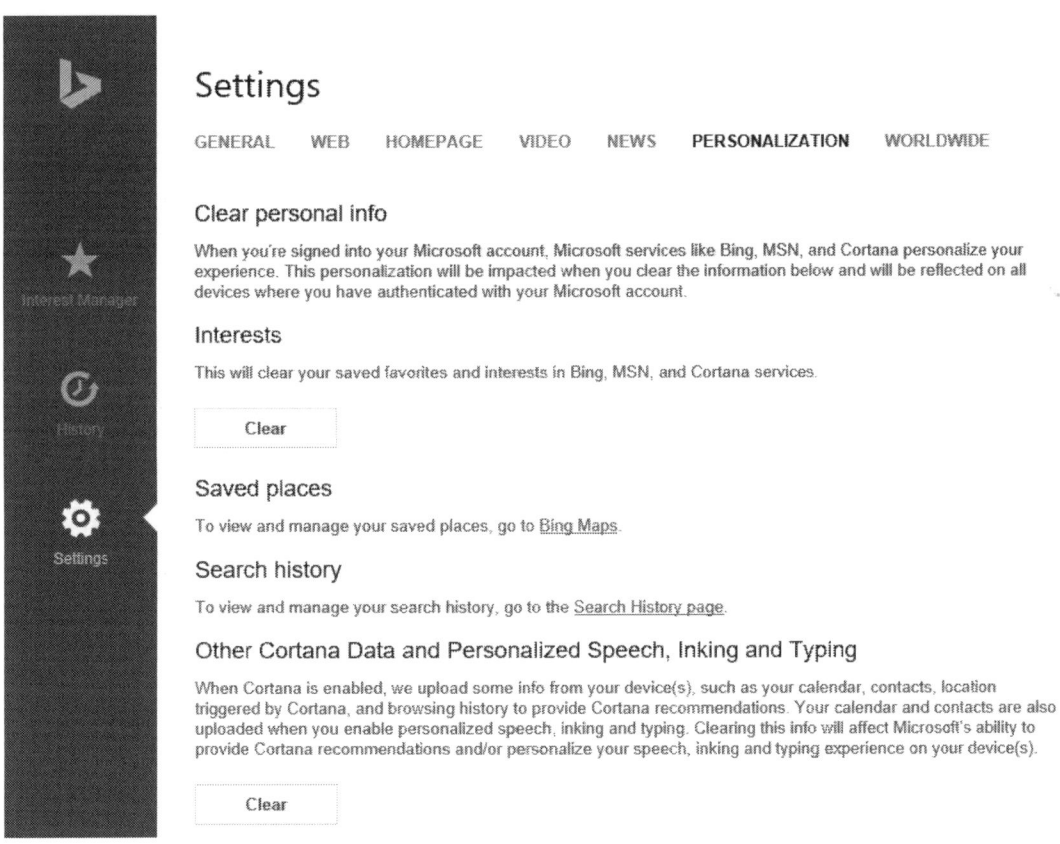

To delete any information that was stored under the Interests or Other Cortana Data and Personalized Speech, Inking and Typing category click on the Clear button located directly under those respective categories.

To remove places that you saved under My Places, click on the ☆ My Places tab located next to the Bing search box.

Click on Edit and select the place(s) under the Home, Work, or Collections category that you'd like to delete. (refer to the screenshot below)

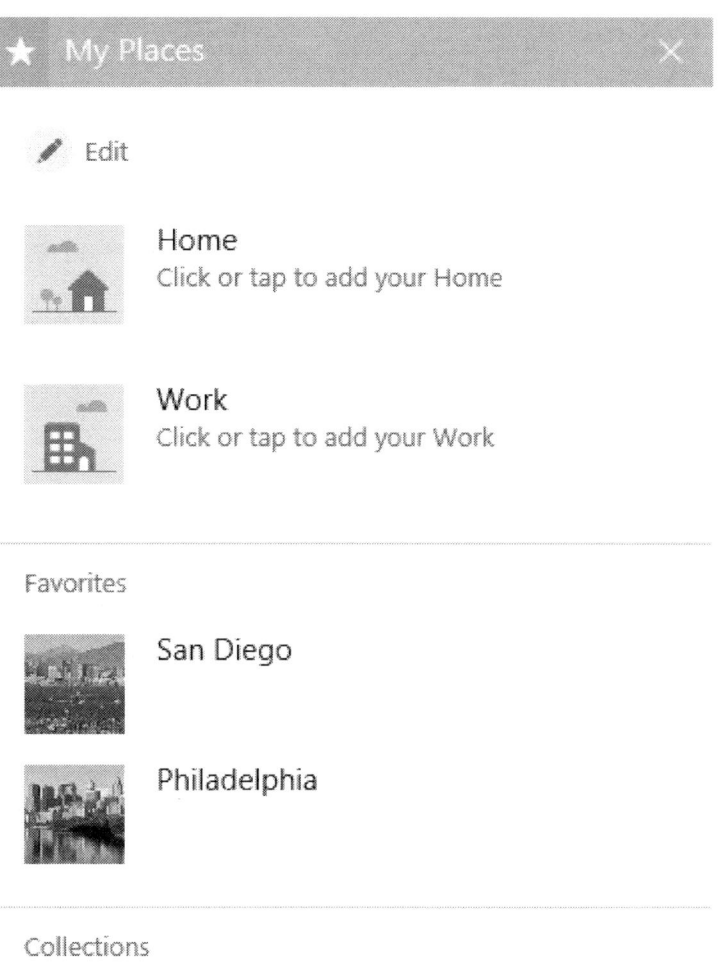

You'll be directed to the following screen to make your changes. (refer to the screenshot below)

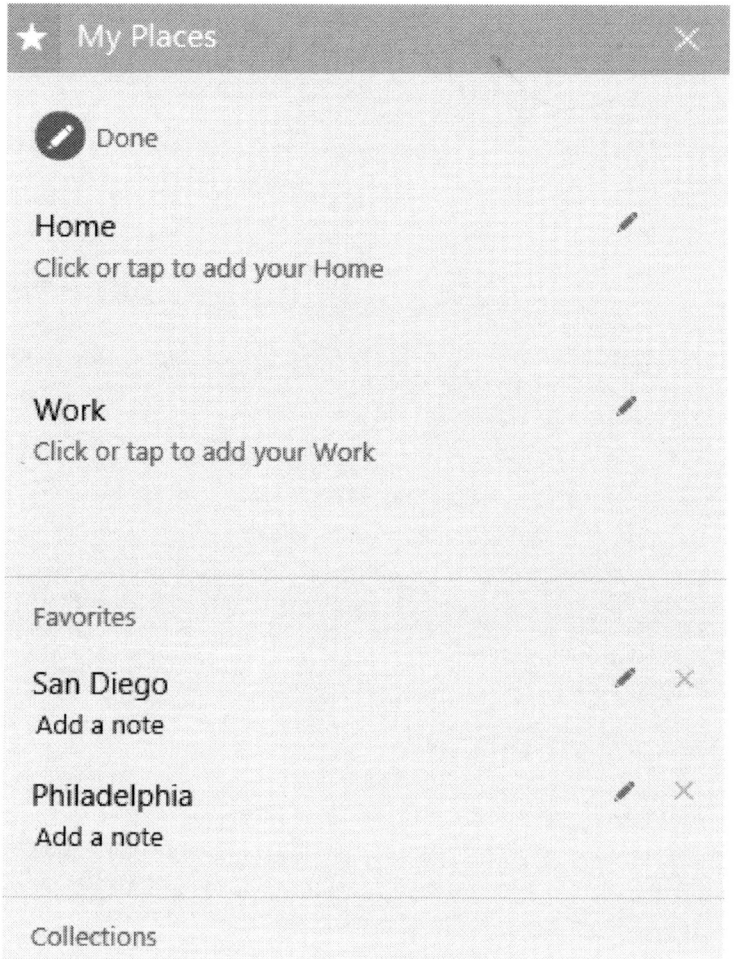

Using the screenshot above as an example, if you wanted to delete your Favorites (San Diego and Philadelphia), you would click on the x next to each place to remove them from your Favorites.

To delete your Search history, go to the Search history page. You can opt to delete single items, or you can clear your entire history. For single items, hover over the item you'd like to remove and click Clear. To clear your entire history, click on the Clear all button. (refer to the screenshot below)

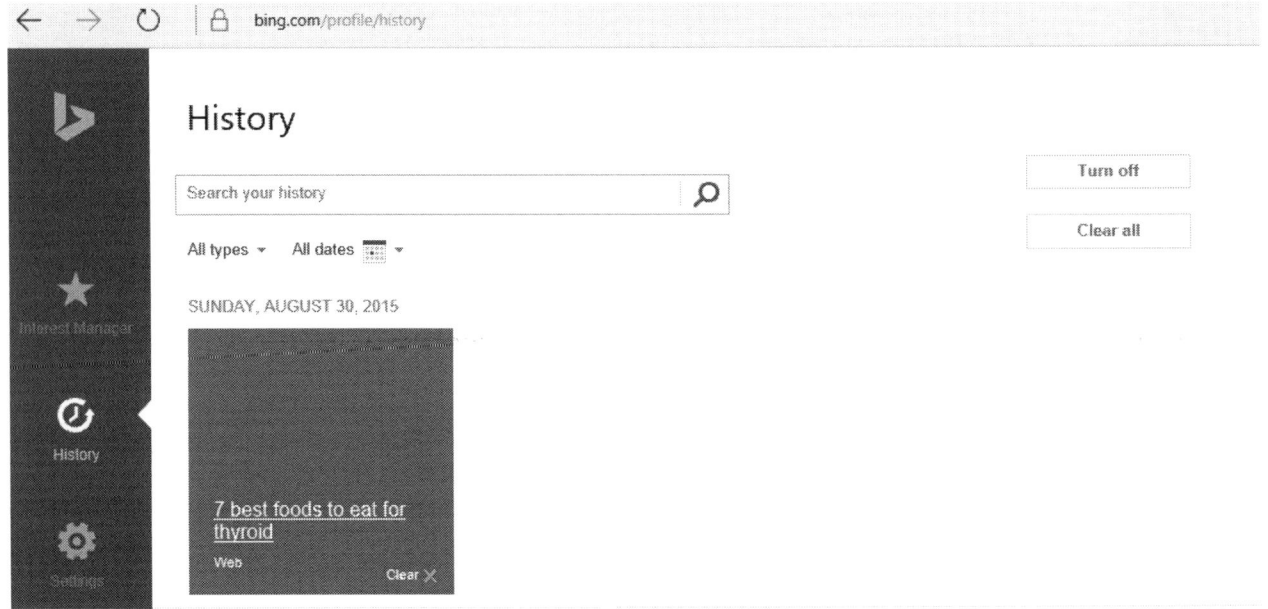

All changes made via the Cortana Notebook will automatically update on the Bing.com dashboard and vice versa.

What type of information does Cortana collect and where is it stored?

Each time you use Cortana it compiles information about you based on your searching history, communication history via messages and apps, contacts, device location and location history, calendar details, and browsing history. All this information is stored on your device in the Cortana Notebook as well as the cloud on the Bing.com dashboard.

Why isn't Cortana talking to me?

In order for Cortana to talk to you, you must ask your question verbally instead of typing it. If you type your question, Cortana would assume that you would like to receive a typed response instead of a verbal one. To ask a question verbally, click on the Mic icon and speak directly into your microphone.

Also, Cortana may not verbally respond to you because your speakers may not be working. To check if your speakers are working, go to Control Panel, then click on Hardware and Sound. (refer to the screenshot below)

> Control Panel

Adjust your computer's settings

View by: Category ▾

 System and Security
Review your computer's status
Save backup copies of your files with File History
Backup and Restore (Windows 7)
Find and fix problems

 Network and Internet
View network status and tasks
Choose homegroup and sharing options

 **Hardware and Sound**
View devices and printers
Add a device
Adjust commonly used mobility settings

 Programs
Uninstall a program

 User Accounts
Change account type

 Appearance and Personalization
Change the theme
Adjust screen resolution

 Clock, Language, and Region
Add a language
Change input methods
Change date, time, or number formats

 Ease of Access
Let Windows suggest settings
Optimize visual display

Under the Devices and Printers heading, click on Device Manager, then click on the arrow next to Sound, video and game controllers to expand its options. (refer to the screenshots below)

 Hardware and Sound

← → ∨ ↑  > Control Panel > Hardware and Sound

Control Panel Home

System and Security
Network and Internet
• **Hardware and Sound**
Programs
User Accounts
Appearance and
Personalization
Clock, Language, and Region
Ease of Access

 Devices and Printers
Add a device | Advanced printer setup | Mouse |  Device Manager
Change Windows To Go startup options

 AutoPlay
Change default settings for media or devices | Play CDs or other media automatically

 Sound
Adjust system volume | Change system sounds | Manage audio devices

 Power Options
Change battery settings | Change what the power buttons do |
Require a password when the computer wakes | Change when the computer sleeps |
Adjust screen brightness

Click on the sound cards listed. Click on the General tab and check the Device status. If you do not see the status listed as "This device is working properly" this may be the issue. (refer to the screenshots below)

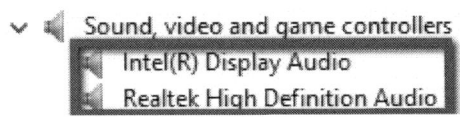

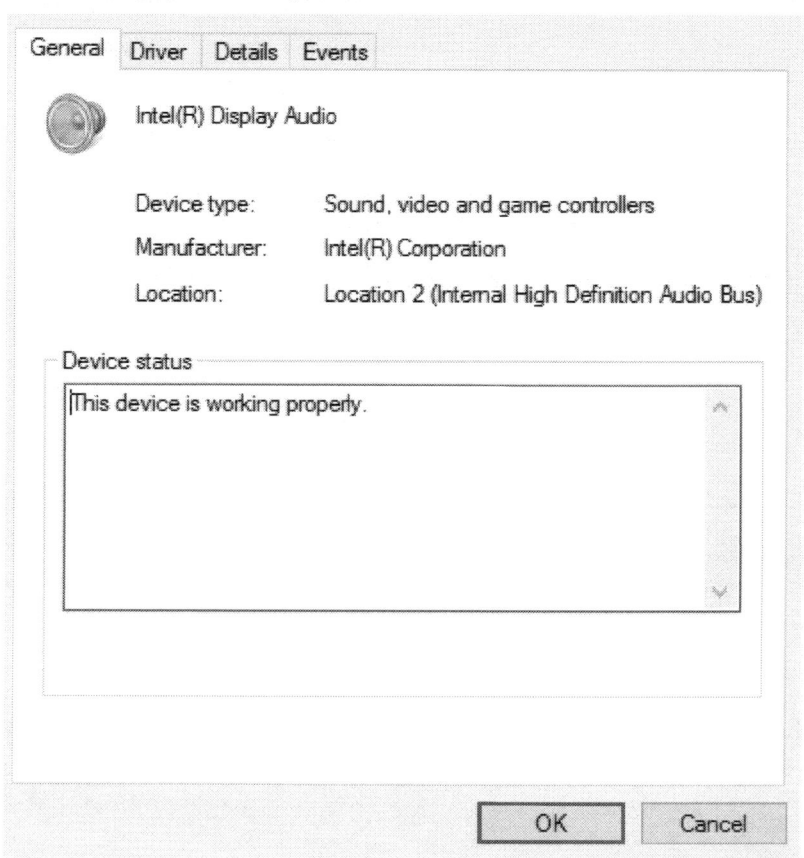

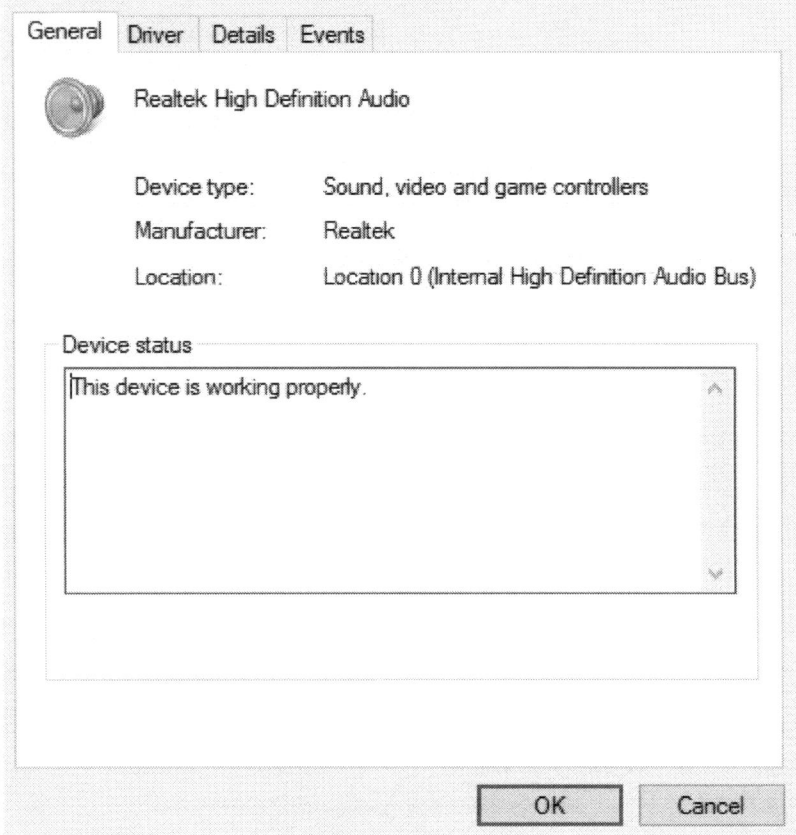

If there are no sound cards listed, or there are yellow question marks in front of the sound cards this may also be a reason as to why your speakers aren't working.

Another reason why Cortana may not respond to you is because your microphone isn't set up. To set up your microphone, go to Control Panel, then click on Ease of Access. (refer to the screenshot below)

Adjust your computer's settings   View by: Category ▾

 System and Security
Review your computer's status
Save backup copies of your files with File History
Backup and Restore (Windows 7)
Find and fix problems

 Network and Internet
View network status and tasks
Choose homegroup and sharing options

 Hardware and Sound
View devices and printers
Add a device
Adjust commonly used mobility settings

 Programs
Uninstall a program

 User Accounts
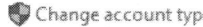 Change account type

 Appearance and Personalization
Change the theme
Adjust screen resolution

 Clock, Language, and Region
Add a language
Change input methods
Change date, time, or number formats

 Ease of Access
Let Windows suggest settings
Optimize visual display

Click on Set up a microphone under the Speech Recognition heading. (refer to the screenshot below)

 Ease of Access Center
Let Windows suggest settings | Optimize visual display | Replace sounds with visual cues
Change how your mouse works | Change how your keyboard works

 Speech Recognition
Start speech recognition | Set up a microphone

Follow the instructions provided. (refer to the screenshots below)

✕

Microphone (Realtek High Definition Audio)

I'll give you a phrase to repeat so I can be sure I'm hearing you correctly. Make sure you're in a quiet place, and your microphone is set up correctly.

Next   Cancel

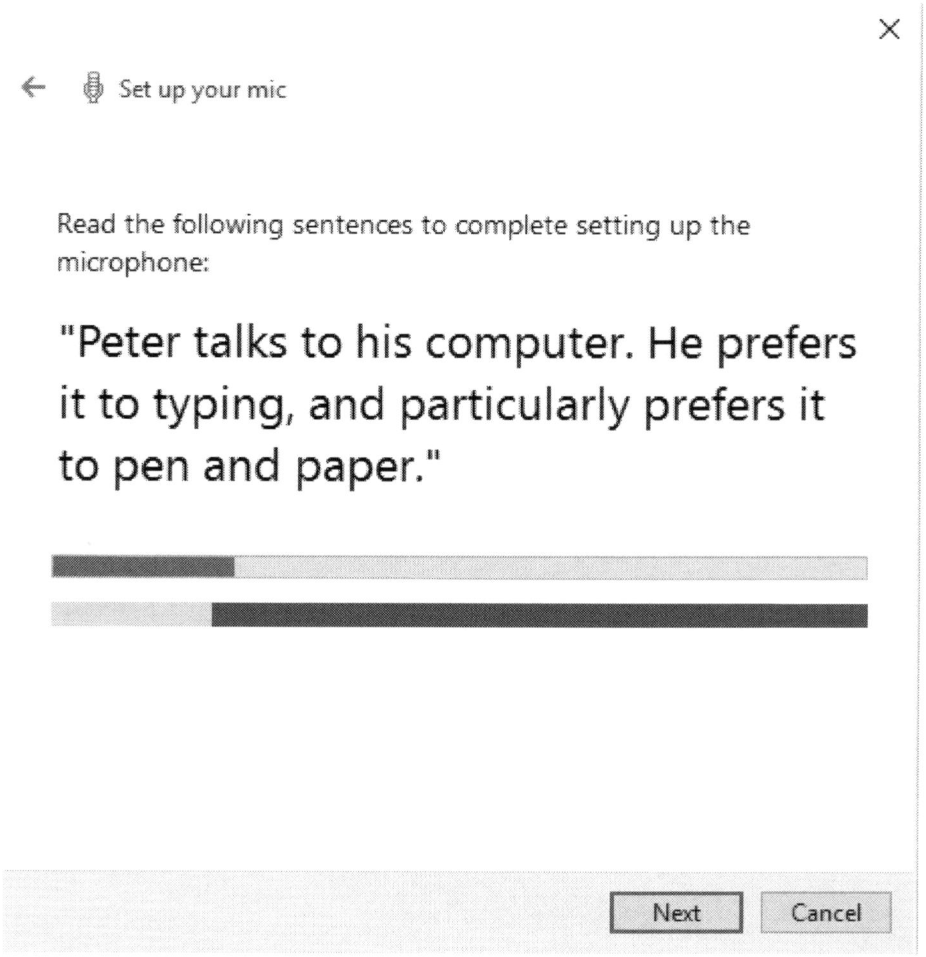

Read the following sentences to complete setting up the microphone:

"Peter talks to his computer. He prefers it to typing, and particularly prefers it to pen and paper."

[Next] [Cancel]

← 🎤 Set up your mic   ✕

Your microphone is now set up.

The microphone is ready to use with this computer. Click Finish to complete the wizard.

[Finish]   [Cancel]

How can I leave feedback about Cortana?

If you'd like to leave feedback about Cortana, click on the Feedback icon  of the Cortana menu. You can choose from three options. These include Ideas, Likes, or Dislikes. After making your selection, type more information regarding your selection into the box. For example, if you selected Likes, you can provide information about the features you liked in Cortana and briefly describe why you liked such features. The information you provide should be no more than 400 characters and should not include any personal information. (refer to the screenshot below)

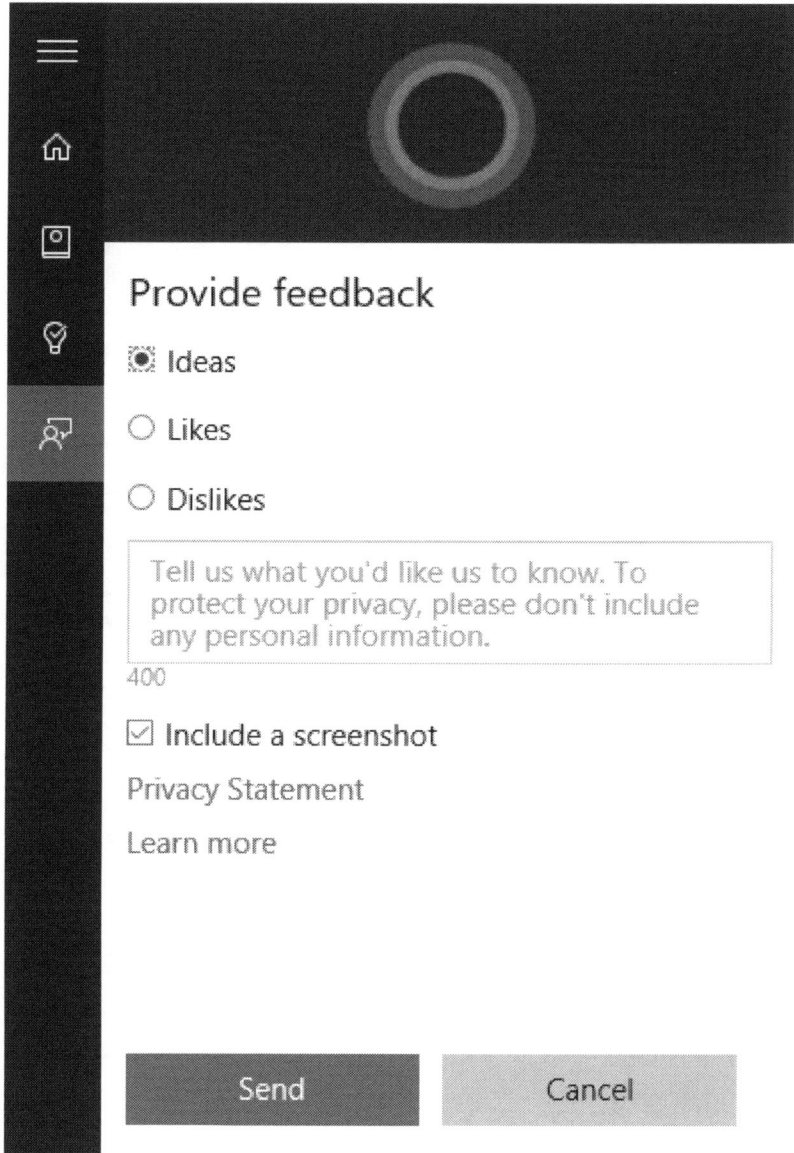

How to View and Delete Browser History in Microsoft Edge?

To view your browser history, click on the Hub icon ☰ . You'll be presented with a list of all the websites you visited without using InPrivate browsing. (refer to the screenshot below)

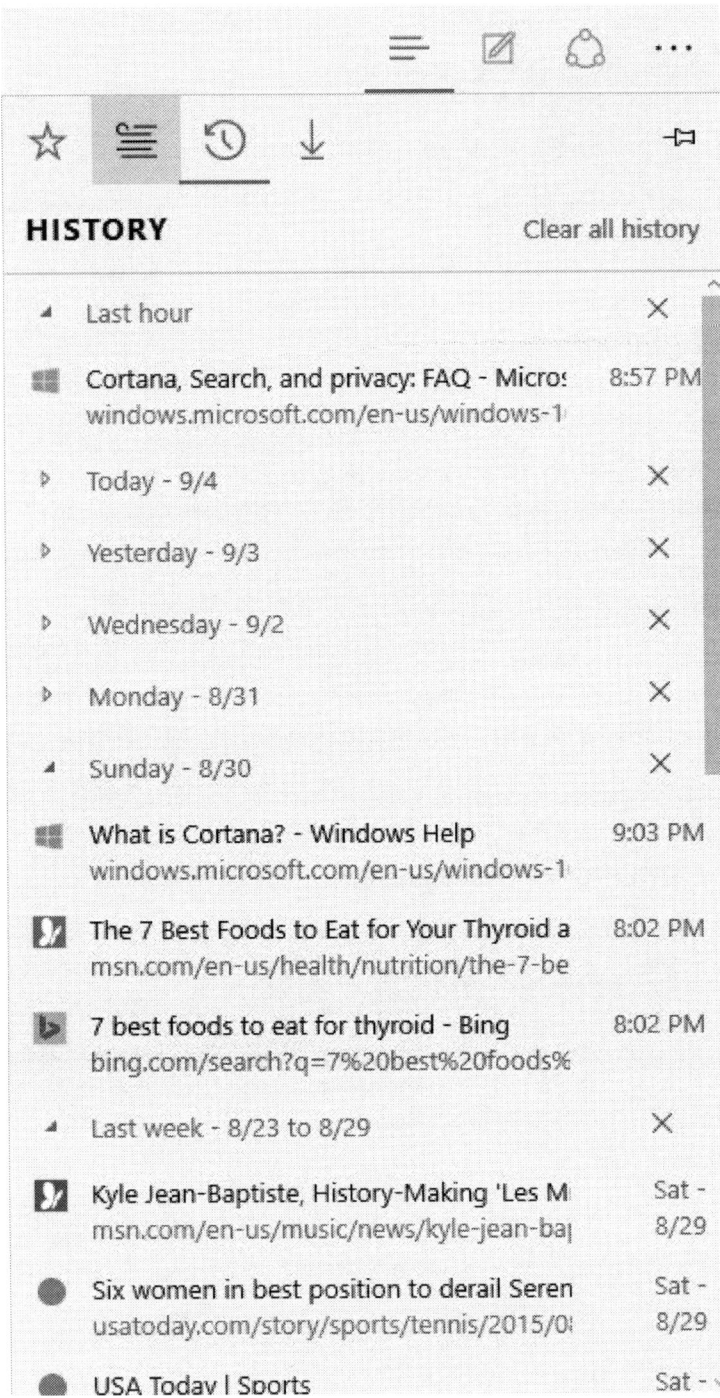

To delete your browser history, click on Clear all history. You'll be presented with the following options: Browsing history, Cookies and saved website data, Cached data and files, Download history, Form data, Passwords, Media licenses, Pop-up exceptions, Location permissions, Full screen permissions, and Compatibility permissions. Select the files you'd like delete from the aforementioned options, then click on the Clear button. (refer to the screenshot below)

☑ Browsing history

☑ Cookies and saved website data

☑ Cached data and files

☐ Download history

☐ Form data

☐ Passwords

Show less ∧

☐ Media licenses

☐ Pop-up exceptions

☐ Location permissions

☐ Full screen permissions

☐ Compatibility permissions

Clear

How to Change the Default Search Engine in Microsoft Edge?

Before you can add a new search engine, you must go directly to its website in order to do so. For example, if you wanted to add Google on your list of search engines, you would open the Microsoft Edge

• • •

browser and go directly to Google.com. Once you're there, go to More actions _____, click on Settings, then click on View advanced settings under the Advanced settings category. Under Search in the address bar with there is a drop down menu with Bing as the default search engine and another option <Add

new> for you to enter the search engine of your choice. (refer to the screenshot below)

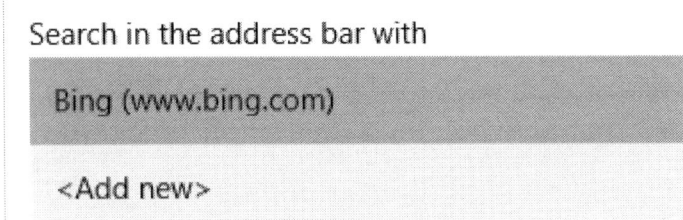

Click on Google and select the option that best suits your needs. If you'd like to make Google your default browser, click on Add as default. If you'd like to add Google to your list of search engine options, click on Add. If you'd like to remove Google from your list of search engine options, click on Remove. (refer to the screenshot below)

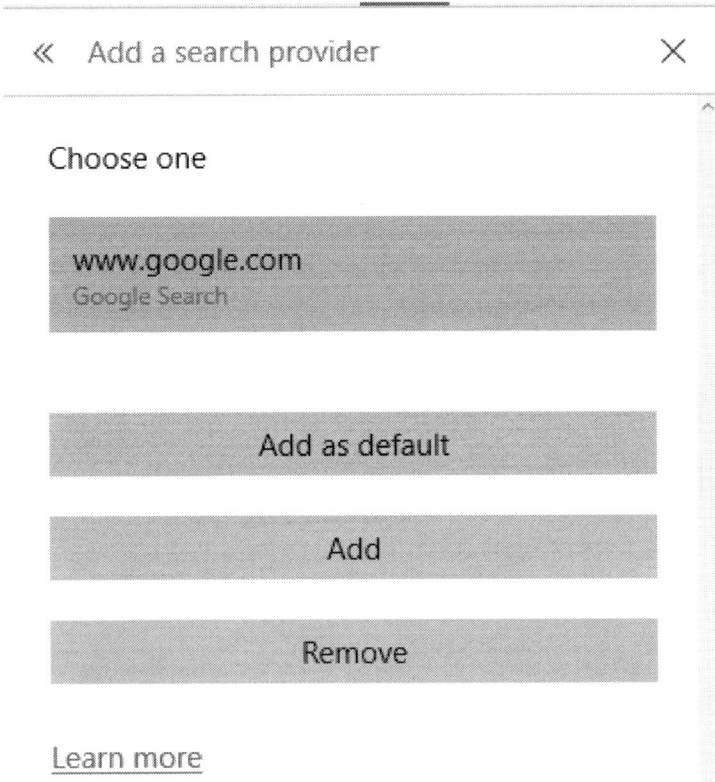

Although you're free to change your default search engine, it is recommended that you leave Bing as your default. By doing so, you'll be provided with a uniformed search experience since Bing was configured to work hand in hand with the Windows 10 operating system. With Bing as your default search engine you'll gain faster access to Windows 10 apps through direct links, you'll receive relevant results from Cortana based on your search queries, and you'll be granted immediate assistance with any issues or concerns you may have with Microsoft Edge or Windows 10.

How to Change the Home Page in Microsoft Edge?

Open your Microsoft Edge browser and click on More actions ⋯ . Under Open with select A specific page or pages. You can choose one of the default options such as MSN or Bing, or you can add a website of your choice. To add your desired website, click on Custom, then enter the web address. (refer to the screenshots below)

Open with

◯ Start page

◯ New tab page

◯ Previous pages

◉ A specific page or pages

| MSN |
| Bing |
| Custom |

| MSN |
| Bing |
| Custom |

about:start ✕

Enter a web address ＋

Each time you open the Microsoft Edge browser you'll be directed to the web address you entered in the Custom field. For example, if you entered eBay in the Custom field, you would be directed to that website each time you open the Microsoft Edge browser.

How can I find out about which version of Microsoft Edge I'm using?

Open your Microsoft Edge browser and click on the More actions icon ⋯ , then click on Settings.

Scroll down to About this app and you'll be provided with information on the version of Microsoft Edge that you're using. (refer to the screenshot below)

About this app

Microsoft Edge 20.10240.16384.0

© 2015 Microsoft

How can I make Microsoft Edge my Default Browser?

Click on the Start button, then click on Settings. (refer to the screenshot below)

Click on System, then select Default apps. (refer to the screenshots below)

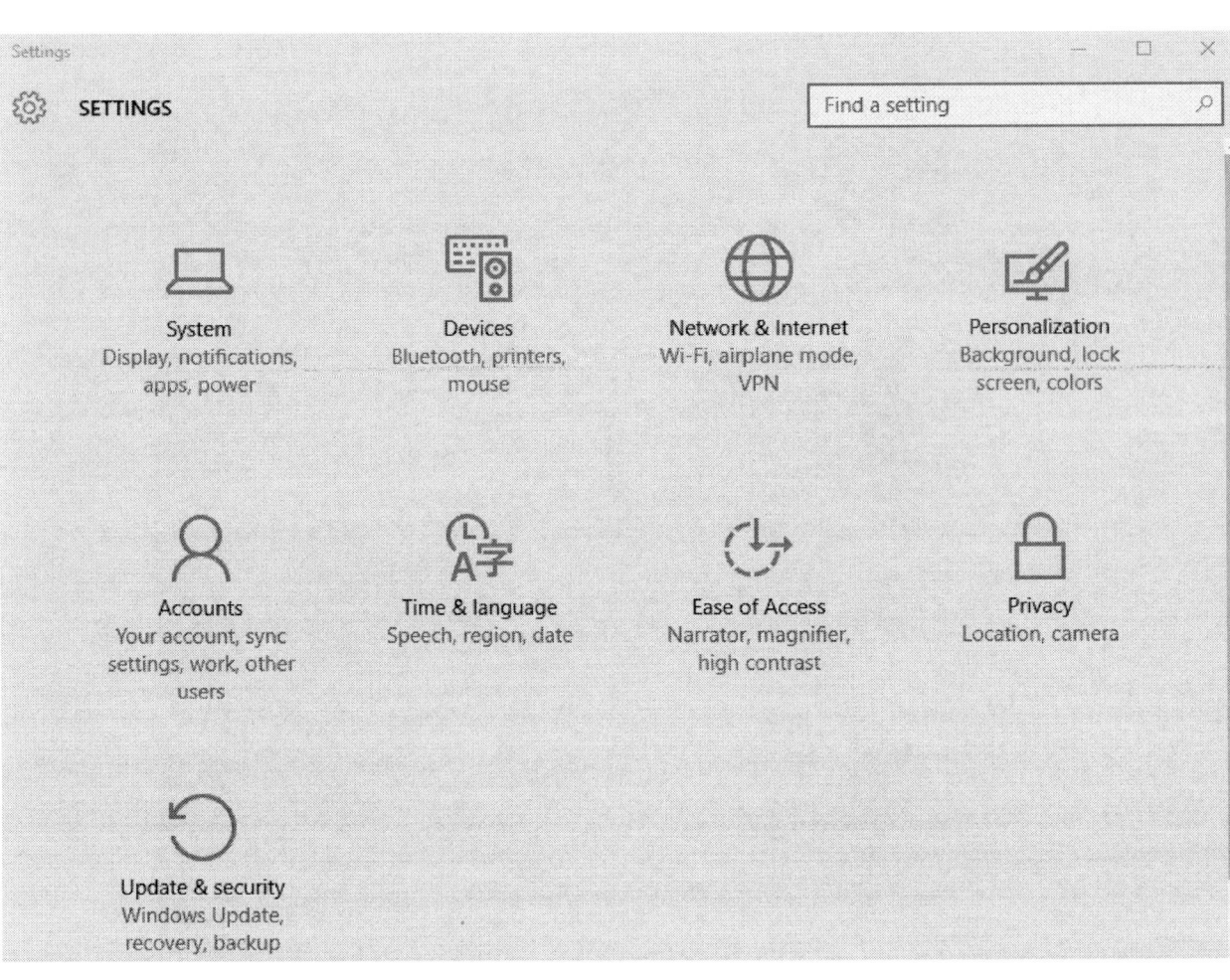

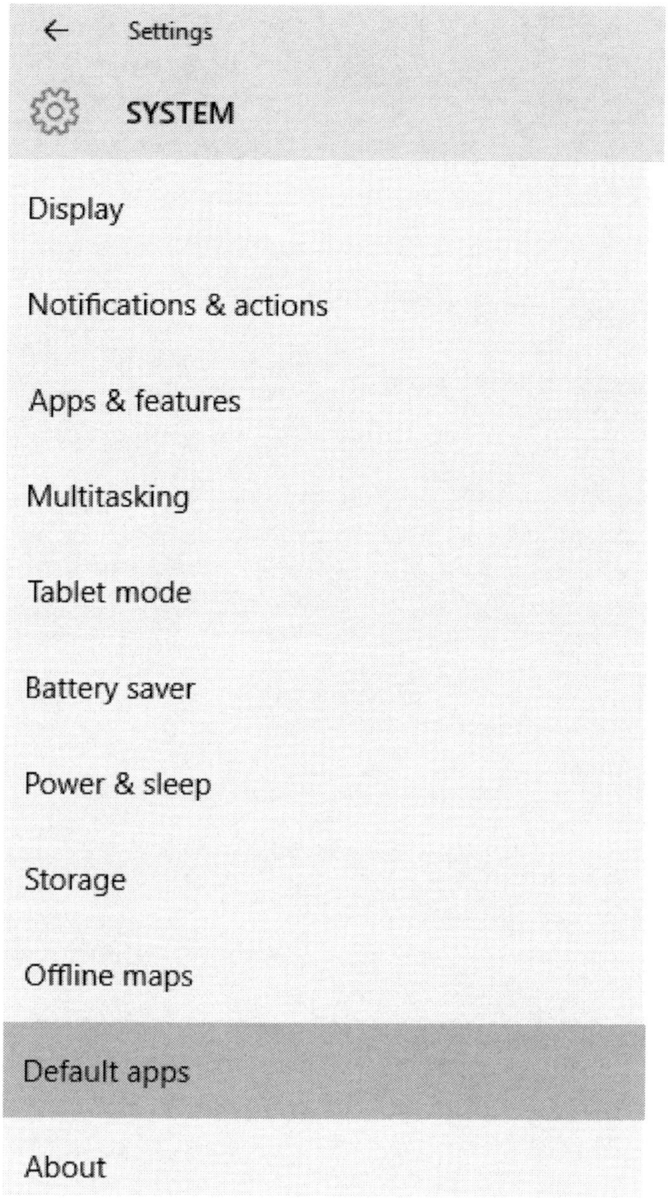
Settings
SYSTEM
Display
Notifications & actions
Apps & features
Multitasking
Tablet mode
Battery saver
Power & sleep
Storage
Offline maps
Default apps
About

Go to Web Browser and click on the browser that is currently set as your default browser. For example, in the screenshot below Google Chrome is set as the default browser. If you'd like to change the default browser to Microsoft Edge, select that option from the list of apps to make it your default browser. (refer to the screenshot below)

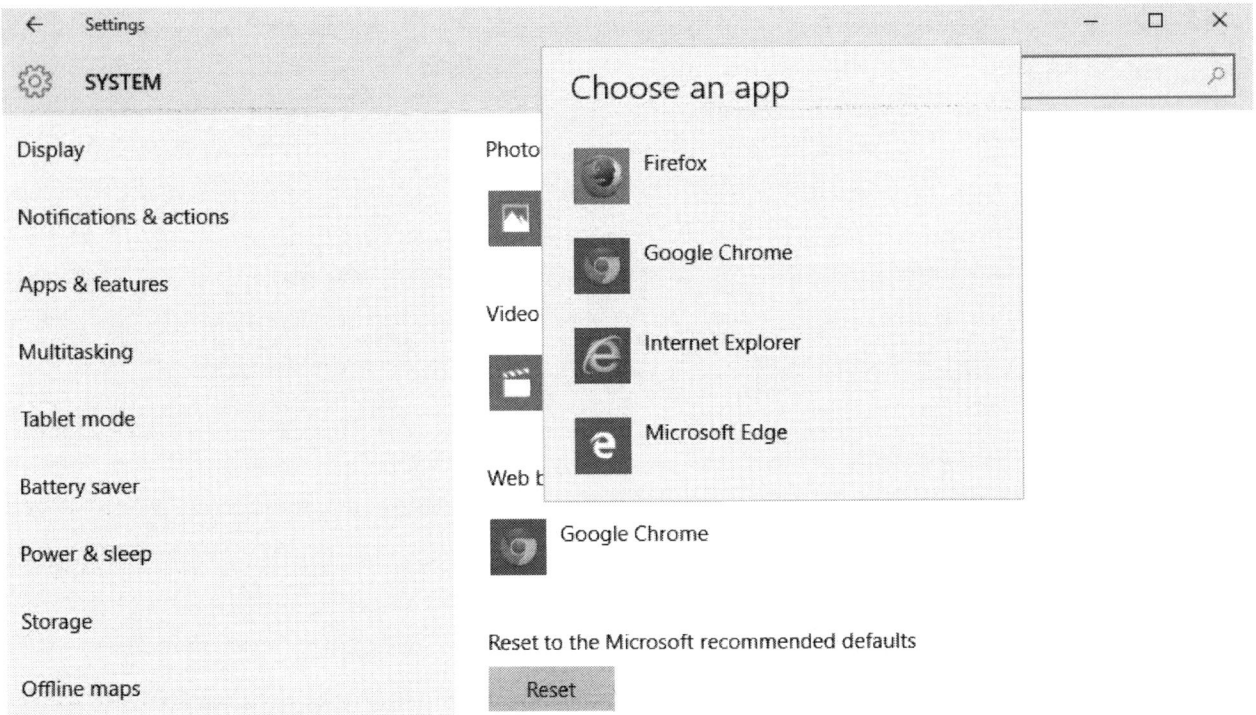

How to AutoComplete Web Forms with Microsoft Edge?

Filling out forms online can often be a tedious process. However, Microsoft Edge has made it easier for its users to fill out forms with its AutoComplete feature. Go to More actions ...., click on Settings, then scroll down to Advanced settings and click on View advanced settings. Scroll down to Save form entries and slide the button to the On position. (refer to the screenshot below)

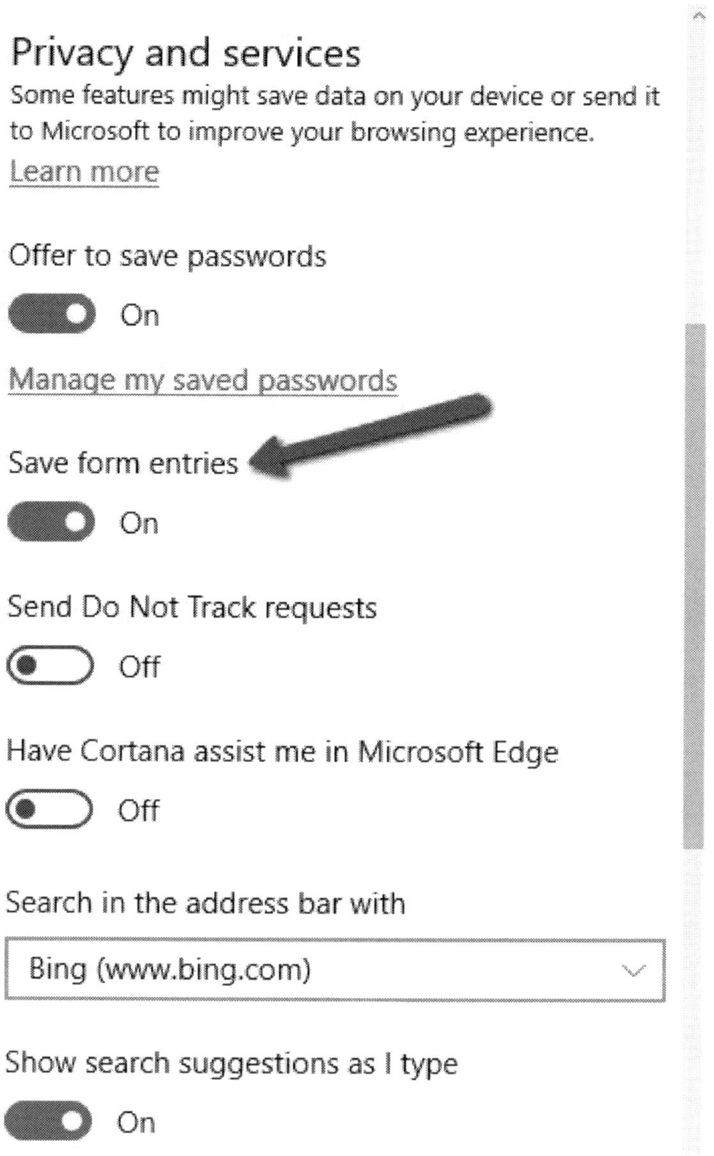

Privacy and services

Some features might save data on your device or send it to Microsoft to improve your browsing experience.
Learn more

Offer to save passwords

O On

Manage my saved passwords

Save form entries ◀━━━━━

O On

Send Do Not Track requests

O Off

Have Cortana assist me in Microsoft Edge

O Off

Search in the address bar with

Bing (www.bing.com)	⌄

Show search suggestions as I type

O On

How can I save passwords in Microsoft Edge?

• • •

Click on the More actions icon _____ , then click on Settings. Scroll down to Advanced settings and click on View advanced settings. Under the Offer to save passwords heading, slide the button to the On position. (refer to the screenshot below)

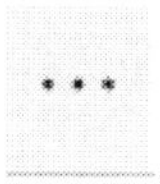

Privacy and services

Some features might save data on your device or send it
to Microsoft to improve your browsing experience.

Learn more

Offer to save passwords

 On

Manage my saved passwords

If you'd like to manage your saved passwords, click on Manage my saved passwords as pictured above.
You'll be presented with a list of all the passwords you were prompted to save in the Microsoft Edge
browser. To delete a saved password, click on the x located directly to the right of the website. (refer to
the screenshot below)

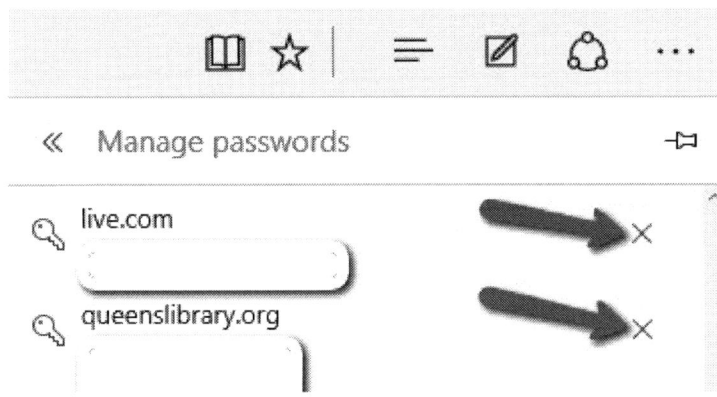

How can I turn off the Pop-ups in Microsoft Edge?

To turn off pop-ups, go to More actions _____, then click on Settings. Click on View advanced settings
under the Advanced settings heading. Under Block pop-ups, slide the button to the On position. (refer to
the screenshot below)

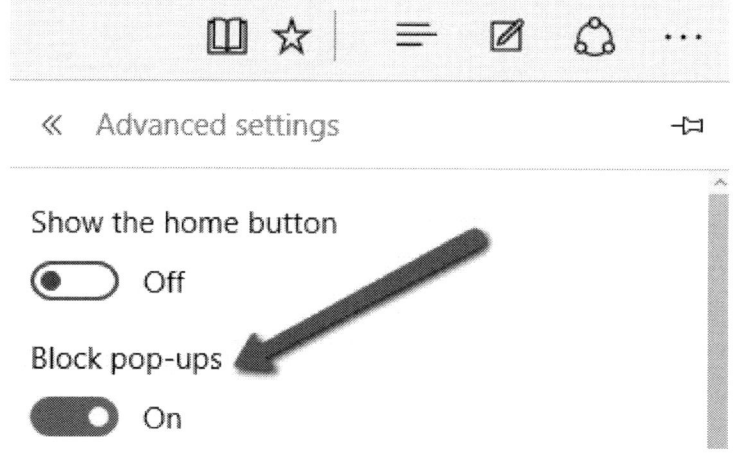

How can I Import my Favorites from another Browser?

To import your Favorites from another browser such as Google Chrome or Internet Explorer, go to More

actions ···, then click Settings. Click on the link Import favorites from another browser. (refer to the screenshot below)

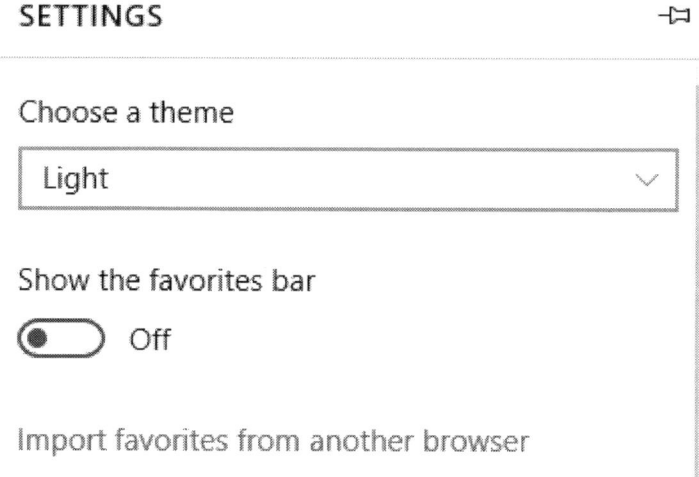

You'll be directed to another screen to select the browsers from which you'd like to have your favorites imported. For example, if you had favorites to be imported from Google Chrome and Internet Explorer, you would check the boxes next to each of those options. Then, you would click Import. (refer to the screenshot below)

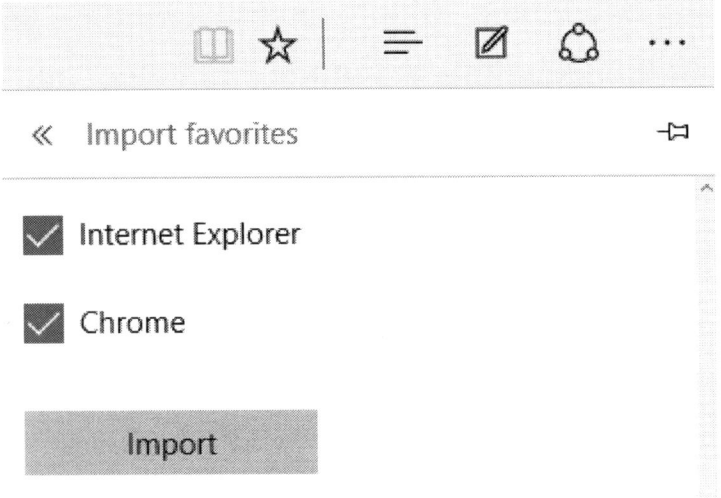

To gain access to your Favorites, click on the Hub icon ☰ , then click on Favorites ☆ . You'll be presented with a screen such as the one below.

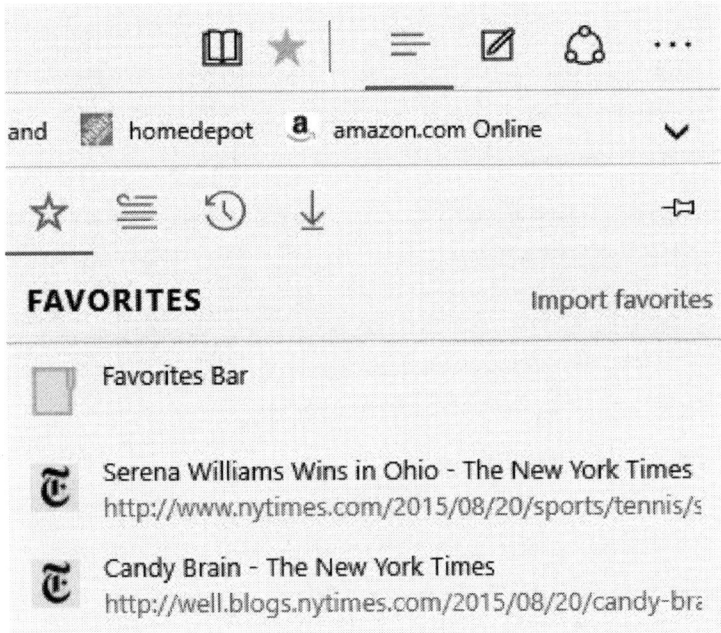

In the Favorites Bar folder, you'll be able to view all the websites or web pages you saved in that specific area. The Favorites Bar appears directly under the address bar and arranges the websites or web pages you saved starting from the left hand side of the screen to the right hand side. The Favorites Bar provides you with quicker access to websites or web pages you frequently visit. Under the Favorites Bar folder in the screenshot above are links to articles in the New York Times which have been saved as Favorites.

The screenshot below shows multiple websites saved on the Favorites Bar.

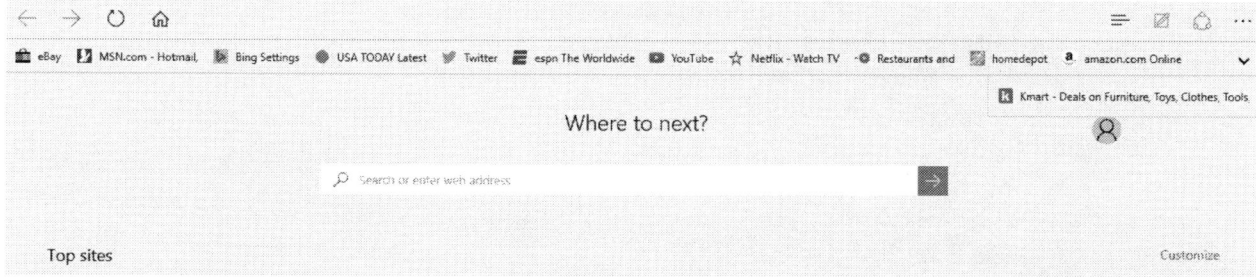

Once the Favorites Bar is filled from the left hand side of the screen to the right hand side, additional websites or web pages are saved on the right hand side directly under the last item that was saved. In the screenshot above, Kmart was placed directly under Amazon. Any additional websites or web pages saved would come directly under Kmart.

To view all the websites or web pages you saved on the Favorites Bar, click on the Hub icon   , select Favorites ☆ , then click on the Favorites Bar folder. (refer to the screenshot below)

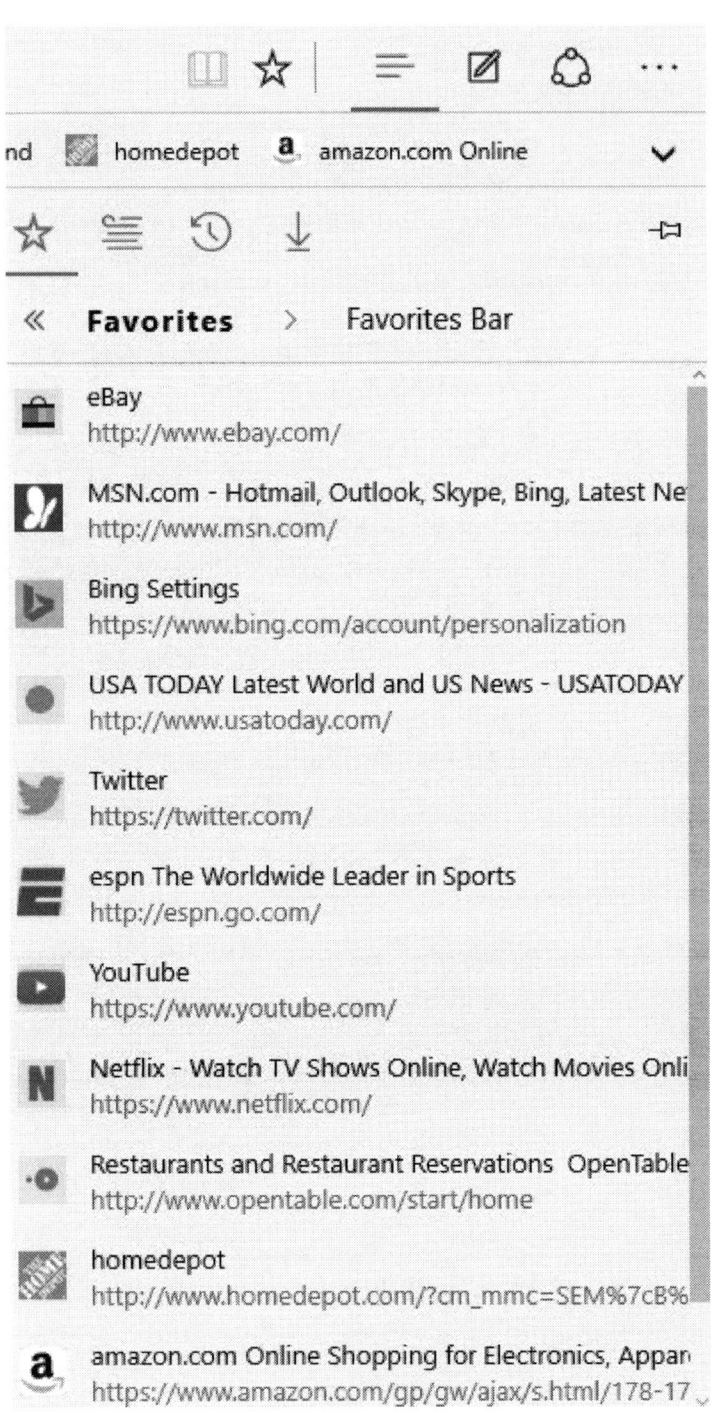

How can I show my Favorites Bar in Microsoft Edge?

To show the Favorites Bar, click on the More actions icon 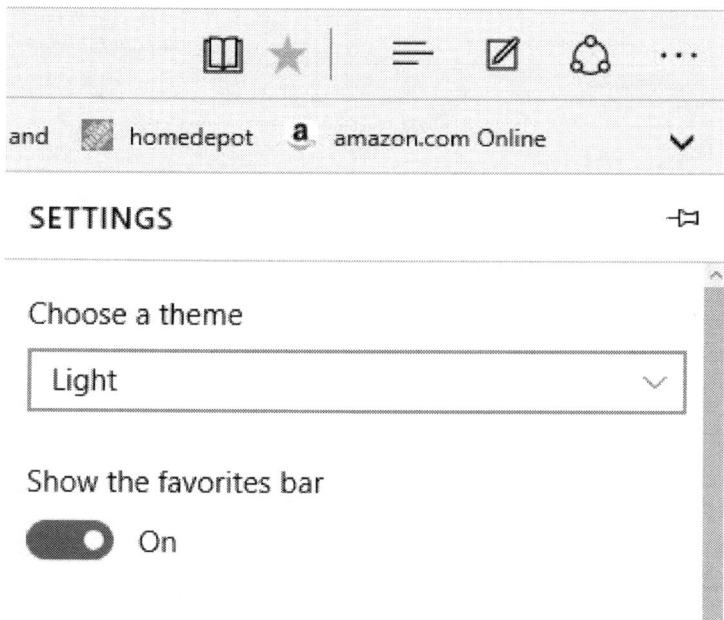, click on Settings, then go to Show the favorites bar and slide the button to the On position. (refer to the screenshot below)

How can I show the Home button in Microsoft Edge?

To show the Home button ⌂ on the address bar of Microsoft Edge, go to More actions ⋯, click on Settings, then click on View advanced settings under the Advanced settings heading. Under Show the home button, slide the button to the On position. (refer to the screenshot below)

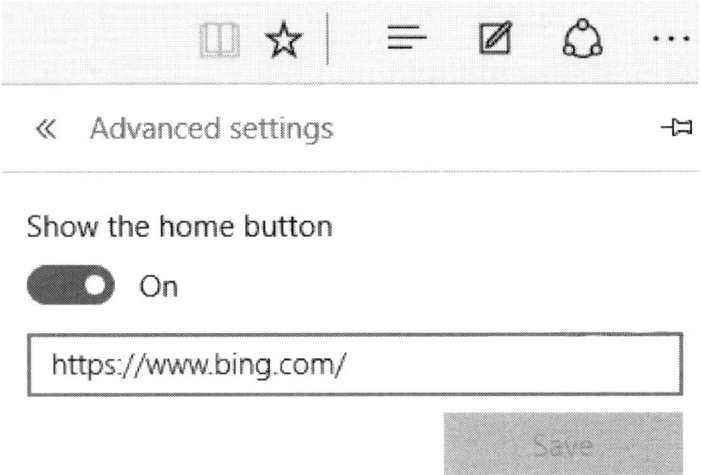

When you click on the Home button 🏠 , by default, it is set to be redirected to the Start page. However, you can change this setting by typing in the desired website to which you'd like the Home button to be redirected. Then, click Save. In the screenshot above, Bing has been entered as the website to which the user would be redirected once the Home button is clicked.

How can I switch from using Microsoft Edge to Internet Explorer?

To switch from Microsoft Edge to Internet Explorer, go to More actions •••, then click on Open with Internet Explorer. (refer to the screenshot below)

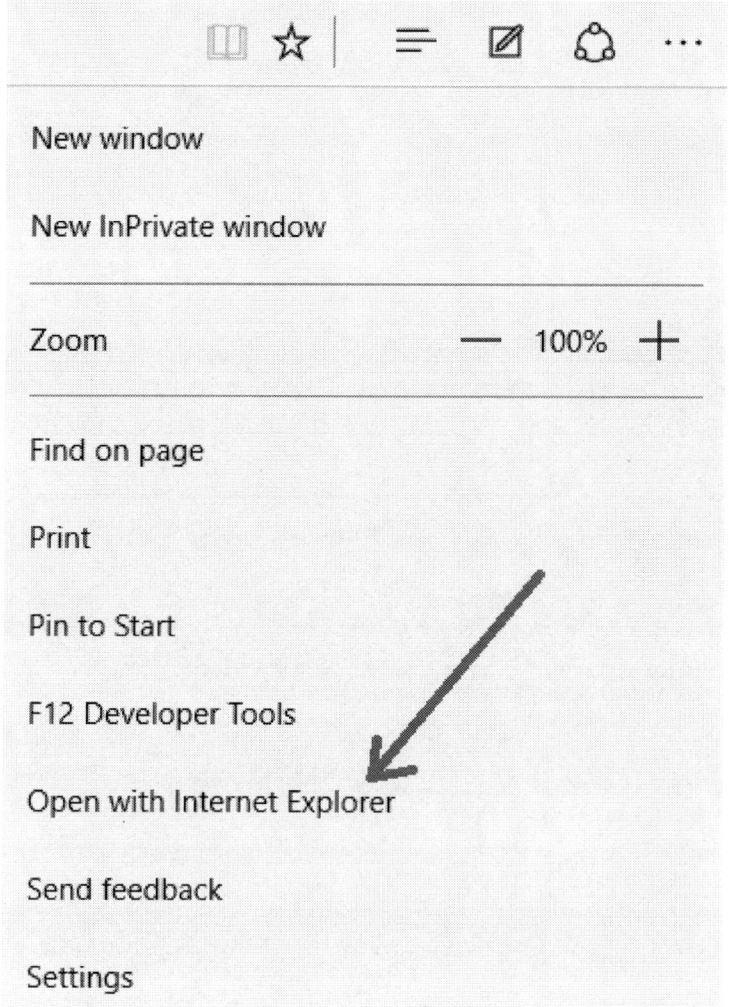

How can I disable Adobe Flash Player?

To disable the Adobe Flash Player, click on the More actions icon , then click on Settings under the Advanced settings heading. Under the heading Use Adobe Flash Player, slide the button to the Off position. (refer to the screenshot below)

Use Adobe Flash Player

⬤⚪ Off

How can I report a problem with a site that I'm using in Microsoft Edge?

To report a problem with a site that you're using in Microsoft Edge, go to More actions _____, then click on Send feedback. You must be on the site to perform this task. For example, if you are browsing through msn.com and you come across an unresponsive web page, you would click on Send feedback.

You'll be presented with the Feedback & reporting screen. On this screen, you would see the URL for the web page being reported and you would be asked to provide more information about the issue. (refer to the screenshot below)

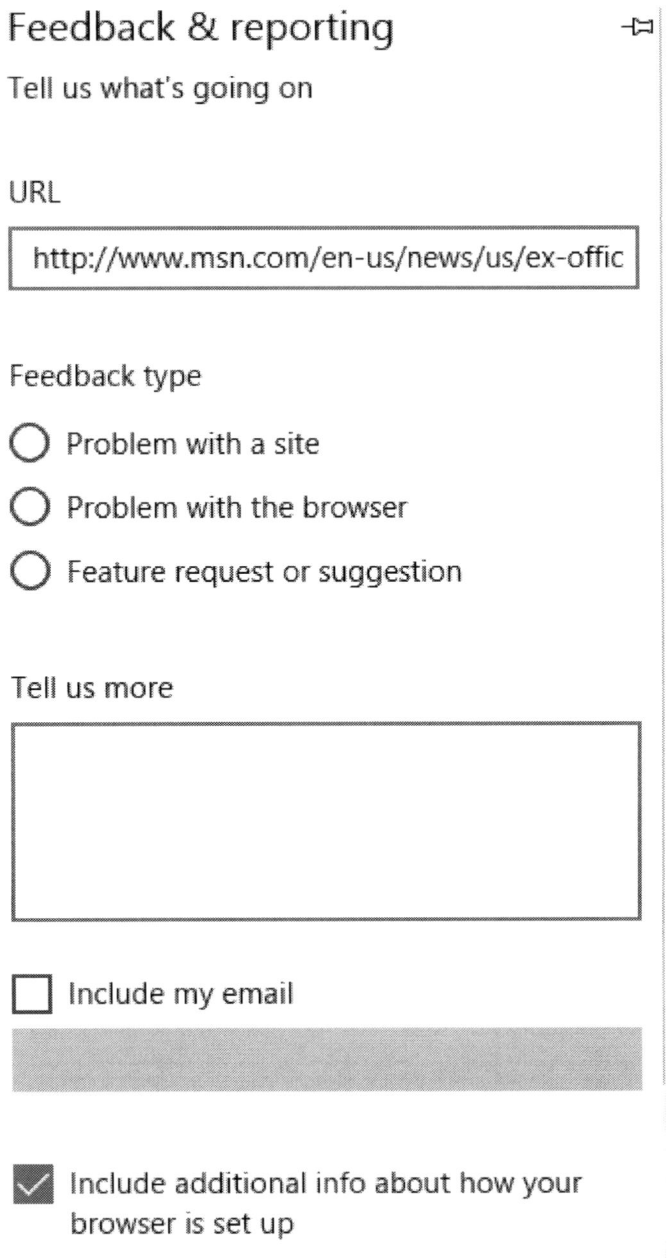

Feedback & reporting

Tell us what's going on

URL

http://www.msn.com/en-us/news/us/ex-offic

Feedback type

◯ Problem with a site

◯ Problem with the browser

◯ Feature request or suggestion

Tell us more

☐ Include my email

☑ Include additional info about how your browser is set up

You can also report a Problem with the browser or provide a Feature request or suggestion as indicated in the screenshot above. Moreover, you can check the Include my email box and type your email address in the field provided. (refer to the screenshot above)

Made in the USA
San Bernardino, CA
24 March 2016